The Men Who Condemned
Jesus Christ

The Men Who Condemned
Jesus Christ

Pilate, Caiaphas and Herod
in Profile

Simon Webb

Also from the Langley Press

What Do We Know About Pontius Pilate?

What Do We Know About Caiaphas?

What Do We Know About Herod Antipas?

In Search of the Celtic Saints

In Search of the Northern Saints

The Theology of Small Things

For free downloads and more from the Langley Press,
please visit our website at

http://tinyurl.com/lpdirect

Contents

Introduction

This book is based on the perhaps rather foolish idea that the stories that are found in the New Testament can be compared to, and studied alongside, the works of both ancient and modern historians, and the findings of archaeologists. My approach here is not, however, to look at the Gospels in particular solely from the historical perspective; but to use a view of them as history alongside other approaches. The problem for anyone attempting this is that there always seem to be many places where the Gospel accounts do not line up with the historical accounts, so that the picture that emerges of both events and characters can seem at the same time complex, incomplete, and rather blurred where the texts seem to be following quite different lines.

Where Pontius Pilate, Joseph Caiaphas and Herod Antipas are concerned, the rather impressionistic, or even cubist, picture that emerges of these men from the sources seems to satisfy certain modern, and even post-modern, ideas of how human character itself should be regarded. What we know about them is jumbled and incomplete; but then can we know more about anyone, even ourselves?

Even readers who stick closely to the texts of the Gospels, and never look at the relevant ancient or modern historians, or at any kind of commentary or archaeological report, will not gain a completely focused view of the events surrounding Christ's Passion. As I hope the following pages will make clear, each of the canonical Gospels include and exclude different aspects of the story, and they sometimes contradict each other in remarkable ways. In Acts, Luke even contradicts at least one important statement he makes in his Gospel.

The differences between the Gospels, and between their accounts and those given in the texts of ancient historians, certainly have something to do with the different outlooks of the various writers involved. The Roman-Jewish historian Josephus, who was born in 37 CE, wrote about many of the figures mentioned in the Gospels, and he even wrote about Jesus, but, unlike the Gospel writers, Josephus showed an almost total lack of interest in the Christian Messiah. His treatment of this figure is so scanty, in fact, that it is likely that later Christian editors of his works adjusted his mentions of Jesus to bring them more into line with their own beliefs.

By contrast, the Gospel writers were, by definition, so committed to Jesus that they could hardly avoid presenting a favourable picture of him. By excluding certain details, tweaking others and interpreting what they themselves had written in certain ways, the Evangelists were not, however, falsifying anything. 'What really happened' was probably not a concern for them at all. They can be thought of as trying to convey not 'facts', but a message.

The sources available to the Gospel writers, and other writers who have tried to cover what they covered, are very different from each other, and in themselves dictate the nature and emphasis of the resulting texts. Starting with a mix of anecdotes, prophesies, inspirations, beliefs, loyalties and probably now long-lost, older and fragmentary texts, Matthew, Mark, Luke and John (or whoever wrote their Gospels) had to construct narratives that satisfied the needs of their nascent Christian communities. The texts that resulted from such a scenario were bound to be different from, say, a report on a rediscovered ossuary or bone-box that may have contained the bones of Joseph Caiaphas, the

Jewish Temple leader at the time of Christ's crucifixion. Such a report will make use not only of various histories old and new, but also earlier archaeological reports of comparable artefacts, as well as the results of a battery of mind-boggling scientific tests.

Inevitably, a report like this will also show signs of having arisen from a post-modern world that is influenced by scientific, humanist, democratic and egalitarian ideas. Likewise, a history such as Josephus's *Jewish Antiquities*, though it emerged from a similar intellectual world to that which produced the Gospels, offers a quite different perspective, because the writer was influenced by his own concern to interest his Gentile readers in the Jews and their history, make the Jews more admirable in his readers' eyes, and also teach his Roman readers how to get along with his ancient people.

This book attempts to view its three main characters from a variety of different angles, as provided by the contrasting ancient, modern and scientific sources and interpretations that are available. One reason why *The Men Who Condemned Jesus Christ* does not include a section on Judas Iscariot, who is often grouped with Pilate, Caiaphas and Herod Antipas, is because the historians, as opposed to the Gospel-writers, who first wrote about these events, paid little attention to him. Although Dante put him in the lowest den of his Inferno, and medieval people were encouraged to think of him as an evil wretch, he was nowhere near as important in the political context of first-century Palestine as Pilate, Caiaphas and Herod Antipas. For this reason, it is difficult to illuminate the biblical Judas by the light of the Judas of the earliest histories.

While sources, influences and audiences play a role, the medium in which a narrative or interpretation appears has a profound influence on its own character and effect. The fact that the oldest extant versions of the Gospels are written in the common street-Greek of the Roman empire gives them a special quality and significance, and speaks volumes about the people who first wrote them, and also about their first readers.

The sometimes very fanciful re-tellings of, and additions to, the stories of the three men who are the subject of this book, that appeared in the Middle Ages in various languages, were likewise influenced by the conventions and expectations of their religious and cultural contexts. The contents of some of these seem to have been dictated by a kind of frustration at the paucity of information about Pilate, Caiaphas and Herod Antipas in the canonical Gospels. The apocryphal gospels, and other works produced by later Christian authors, sought to answer such questions as, how did Pilate die? What happened to his wife? What about his children?

Sometimes these medieval treatments show historical insight, imagination and a surprising amount of sympathy for these men, who are supposed to occupy a very low position in the Christian moral universe. As in the case of the fanciful later stories that were attached to the Three Kings, these medieval treatments of the men who condemned Jesus offer interpretations of their characters, explain many modern-day attitudes to them, and offer insights into the intellectual worlds that created the texts. At times, for instance, very medieval ideas such as the role of the knight and the attitude to Jews, Muslims and the lands to the south and east of Europe make themselves evident in these accounts.

In the same way, a dramatic treatment of the story of the death of John the Baptist, written at first in French prose poetry by a decadent, English-speaking, Victorian Irishman is bound to be different from the Gospel treatments, the account of these events given by Josephus, and versions produced during the Middle Ages.

In my analyses of how the characters of Pilate, Caiaphas and Herod Antipas have been depicted in film and on TV, I have tried to show how the nature and content of such screen presentations are influenced by the practicalities of the relevant media, and the perceived expectations of their audiences. Although, like the many novelizations of New Testament events, 'Jesus films' can be trivial, exploitative and annoying, they can have a wide influence, particularly among people who would never dream of sitting down and reading the Gospels. They are also a source of interpretations and insights, and can reflect the cultural contexts in which they were produced in a fascinating way.

The role of this book, which brings together profiles of Pilate, Caiaphas and Herod Antipas that were previously published as separate volumes, is not to present final or definitive views of any of these men. It is to explore what is known about them, and what can be inferred about them from the evidence, and also to explore to some extent how they have been seen and represented down the centuries. Of course there are already books about all three of them, but as the flow of modern accounts, and particularly archaeology, develops, changes and gathers more evidence and ideas, there may be value in a new attempt to take stock from a particular viewpoint.

From the viewpoint of 2018, the lessons that can perhaps be drawn from what we know about Pilate, Caiaphas and Herod Antipas could be said to concern important issues around communication, culture-clash and fear: all important concerns in today's world.

Even if all the characters involved in the Passion narrative were fluent in a common language, communication across such diverse cultures was always going to be a problem. Although figures like Josephus and the Herods tried to prosper on patches of common ground snatched from each side, it was always going to be difficult for the Pagan culture of the Romans and Greeks to rub along with the ancient monotheistic culture of the Jews.

An example of an attempt to exploit the mismatch

between these world views is seen in the Gospels, where Jesus' accusers translate the very Jewish term 'Messiah' into 'King of the Jews' for Pilate's consumption. Unable, perhaps, to understand that some Jews see Jesus as the Messiah, and probably unclear as to what a Messiah is supposed to be, Pilate views the more political and universal concept of a king as something much more threatening. The Romans don't want a King of the Jews to arise, except on their terms. Jesus, the battered, bleeding king-in-waiting, is a threat and a source of fear and not, as he might have been if understood to be a Messiah, a kind of folksy high-priest of the people.

This attempt by Jesus' accusers to exploit language and cultural differences is sophisticated and remarkably modern. In today's slang, they 'know what buttons to press' when it comes to the Roman Governor of Judea, and they press them with skill. What gives their curve-ball an extra touch of deadly top-spin is the *fear* that underlies the whole business. Although when a threat is perceived to be present, it behoves the threatened to both see and think clearly, all too often fear itself narrows and distorts perception and leads to tragic action. Everything appears black and white, while simultaneously the fearful and threatened also see red. Many of the tragic scenes that are being acted out on the world stage today seem to arise out of perceptions narrowed by fear. In this and many other respects, the actions of the representatives of the diverse cultures present in first-century Palestine seem remarkably modern. The accusers of Jesus who turned their understanding of what he was into the crude, provocative phrase 'King of the Jews' were the true ancestors of the modern pedlars of fake news and divisive, panic politics.

The people of Judea no doubt feared Pilate, and he probably feared what they could do to his life and his future career. The Temple priests, Sadducees most of them, no doubt feared and were very suspicious about the other sects, such as the Essenes and Pharisees, and also the adherents to the oral, folk Judaism of the remoter regions. No doubt everybody sometimes entertained fears about the Messiah whom some expected. What would he do? Whom would he raise up? Whom would he cast down? Whom would he condemn?

For the most part, it seems, the Jesus of the New Testament is without fear, and his comments reflect a perfect understanding of what is going on, and the characters of everyone who is involved. His particular brand of wisdom seems to be beyond human wisdom, but perhaps by at least trying to aspire to possess just a little portion of it, we can see more clearly, banish fear and hate, and embrace peace.

SW, Durham, August 2018

What Do We Know About
Pontius Pilate?

1. Pilate's Mountain

In a forgotten Victorian novel called *A Comedy of Masks*, Mrs Sylvester, very much an English lady abroad, complains that Pilate's Mountain is far too near where she is staying, so that she feels she cannot get away from it. One might think that Mrs Sylvester is staying in the Holy Land, that her holiday is partly a Christian pilgrimage, and that she has been visiting such ancient sights as Caesarea and Jerusalem. In fact Mrs Sylvester and her compatriots are staying at Lucerne in Switzerland, and Mount Pilatus, where some say Pontius Pilate is buried, can be seen from that city.

If nothing else, the story that a mountain in Switzerland is the final resting place of the man who sentenced Jesus to death is a reminder of one of the simultaneously familiar and surprising facts about the history of the Christian religion: the fact that, although it originated in the Middle East, Europe was the main stronghold of Christianity for hundreds of years. When Islam began to be the dominant religion of much of the Middle East, North Africa and even Spain, the area dominated by Christianity became even more concentrated. The religion exists now in the Americas, Africa, and elsewhere outside of Europe because European settlers brought their religion with them, and European missionaries worked hard to convert the locals.

Mount Pilatus is not the only place in Europe that lays claim to Pontius Pilate's remains. Mount Vettore in Italy makes a similar boast, and there we also find Pilate's Lake, underneath which the one-time Roman Prefect of Judea is said to be buried. As we shall see, Lausanne also considers herself a candidate for the title of last home of Pilate.

We might read such legends as attempts to Europeanise the story of Jesus, no part of which, according to the gospels, happened in Europe. Other attempts would include claims that the earthly remains of the Wise Men who visited the new-born Christ at Bethlehem lie at Cologne in Germany, and that the house where the Virgin Mary spent her childhood was miraculously transported from Nazareth to Loreto in Italy near the end of the thirteenth century.

Attempts to link Pontius Pilate, a central character in the Passion narrative, to Europe stand, however, on firmer ground than, for instance, old tales of the Ark of the Covenant being stored in a secret chamber in Rome, or of Jesus visiting Cornwall with Joseph of Arimathea. Pontius Pilate was almost certainly a European, a Roman citizen and an Italian, who lost his position as prefect of Judea and probably returned to, and died in, some part of Europe. Part of the fascination of this enigmatic character is the fact that he is the only named European present in Judea who had a role in the drama of the trial and execution of Christ. It seems that his status as a European caught up in these events may be central to both his notoriety in the eyes of some, and the sympathy with which he is viewed by others.

2. Pilate in Matthew, Mark and Luke

As simultaneously familiar and surprising as the way Christianity survived and flourished partly by moving west from the Holy Land into Europe is the fact that the basic story of Christianity – the life-story of Jesus Christ – has been conveyed for nearly two thousand years via four different accounts: the gospels of Matthew, Mark, Luke and John. Much longer books than the present volume have been written about the differences and similarities between these gospels. The questions of which is the oldest, which the most authoritative; and the relationship between these books and other texts, such as older sources that are now lost, have been debated back and forth for centuries.

Most scholars now divide the gospels into two groups: the so-called synoptic gospels of Matthew, Mark and Luke; and John, which is felt to belong in a class of its own. The figure of Pontius Pilate appears in all four but, true to John's character as the exceptional gospel, the treatment of Pilate is quite different here, though the synoptic gospels also differ from each other in their accounts of the man said to lie under Pilate's Lake.

The shortest gospel, which is thought by many scholars to have been the first written, is Mark. In this gospel, the prelude to Jesus' encounter with Pilate is his night-time arrest or capture by 'a crowd armed with swords and clubs, sent from the chief priests, the teachers of the law, and the elders' (14:43). In other words, Jesus has been captured in the name of the Jewish hierarchy, and the crowd are able to identify him because Judas kisses him: a pre-arranged sign.

According to Mark, Jesus is then taken straight to an impromptu court comprising 'the high priest, and all the chief priests, the elders and the teachers of the law' (14:53). Here witnesses testify against Jesus, but their accounts do not tally. Some unnamed people then give false testimony, saying that they had heard Jesus say he would 'destroy this temple made with human hands and in three days will build another, not made with hands' (14:58), but even these lying witnesses' accounts do not tally.

At last the High Priest questions Jesus, asking for his response to the testimony they have all heard. Meeting nothing but silence from the Nazarene, the High Priest asks him directly, 'Are you the Messiah, the Son of the Blessed One?' (14:61). Jesus' reply causes the High Priest to resort to the ancient Jewish gesture of tearing his clothes – an expression of grief usually associated with bereavement. Jesus claims that yes, he is indeed the Messiah, and that 'you will see the Son of Man sitting at the right hand of the Mighty One and coming on the clouds of heaven' (14:62).

The High Priest sees this statement as blasphemy, and in response, the assembled officials declare that Jesus deserves to die. They spit on him, beat him and cover his head; and the guards who lead Jesus off beat him some more.

It is only after this encounter with the High Priest and the Jewish authorities that, according to Mark's account, Jesus is taken to Pilate. The Prefect kicks off their interview with the question, 'Are you the King of the Jews?' (15:2). This is a phrase (or perhaps we should say title) that, like Pilate's name, has not previously occurred in the Gospel of Mark. Is it Pilate's attempt to translate the word 'Messiah', that the High Priest had perhaps used? Certainly, at this time the Jewish conception of the long-awaited Messiah was a kingly figure, so the use of the phrase 'King of the Jews' as a translation seems reasonable.

Jesus' response to Pilate's question, which seems very abrupt in the context of Mark, may imply that Jesus was himself aware of the way that, between his time with the High Priest and his confrontation with Pilate, the word 'Messiah' has somehow become the phrase 'King of the Jews'. 'You have said so,' says Jesus (15:2). E.V. Rieu, in his 1950s translation for Penguin, renders Jesus' reply as 'The words are yours'; and the King James Bible gives us 'Thou sayest it', which is pretty close to a literal translation of the New Testament Greek.

Pilate may have felt that he had to translate the term 'Messiah', which comes from a Hebrew word meaning 'anointed', because he was talking to Jesus in Greek. Although Pilate's own mother-tongue was probably Latin, Greek, the language in which the New Testament has come down to us, was the *lingua franca* of Rome's Mediterranean empire, built as it was on the foundations of the earlier empire of the Greeks.

Like the unnamed high priest who had questioned Jesus earlier, Pilate is also frustrated by Jesus' decision not to speak in his own defence against the charges brought against him.

In Mark, this first meeting between Pilate and Jesus is immediately followed by an account of the Prefect conversing with a crowd in front of his palace. The crowd is there because the people want to ask Pilate to release a prisoner, as the gospels tell us was the custom at Passover. Pilate offers them 'The King of the Jews', because he knows that the Jewish hierarchy want Jesus killed out of envy; but the crowd cry out for Barabbas instead, described in this gospel as a murderous rioter. In Verse 11 Mark makes it clear that the Jewish elders have previously persuaded the people to ask for Barabbas and not Jesus. Pilate asks what they want him to do with the King of the Jews if he releases Barabbas instead, and they cry out 'Crucify him!' When

Pilate asks them what crime Jesus has committed, the crowd merely bawl back 'Crucify him' again (15:14).

This is perhaps the most chilling moment in Mark's account. The crowd is asked a simple question, which it refuses to answer, offering only a call for violence. The moment might stand as a warning about all those times when fear, anger, prejudice, blind obedience or blood-lust blank out reason and justice.

Straight after this, Mark's Pilate hands Jesus over to be crucified.

The whole of Mark's treatment of Pilate's encounter with Jesus takes up only fifteen verses of one chapter and, not surprisingly, it is lacking in detail. There is no adequate explanation of who Pilate is, what he is doing in Jerusalem, or why the Jewish hierarchy feel compelled to bring Jesus, their prisoner, before him. We only know by implication where Pilate's encounter with the mob takes place, because Mark tells us that the soldiers who took Jesus away led him inside a court or praetorium (15:16), which suggests that Pilate's encounter with the mob, at least, happened outside that building. As we have seen, Mark does not name any of the temple officials who interrogate Jesus in his Chapter 14: likewise he only gives Pilate half of his name, missing off the 'Pontius'. In Mark, Pilate only asks Jesus two questions, one of which Jesus does not answer. After Pilate has handed Jesus' body over to Joseph of Arimathea for burial, Pilate's appearances in Mark come to an end.

In the Gospel of Matthew, the decision of the Jewish hierarchy to send Jesus to Pilate provokes Judas, suddenly stricken with guilt, to try to return the thirty pieces of silver he was paid to hand Jesus over. If nothing else, this provides a break between the morning meeting where the Jewish hierarchy decide to hand Jesus over to Pilate, and Jesus' appearance before the Prefect. It also gives an enhanced sense of the seriousness of the decision of the hierarchy to hand Jesus over: Judas for one assumes that Jesus is now facing death as a result.

In the Gospel of Matthew, we learn that Pilate is 'the governor', although Matthew does not give us his full name (the King James Version adds 'Pontius' here). Pilate asks Jesus roughly the same two questions he asks in Mark, and again Jesus does not answer the second, which is really not so much a question as Pilate's attempt to persuade Jesus to defend himself: 'Don't you hear the testimony they are bringing against you?' (27:13)

As in Mark, Pilate's conversation with the crowd which has gathered to beg for the customary release of a prisoner at Passover follows straight after Jesus refuses to answer his second question; but in Matthew we learn that, during this discussion, the Prefect sits 'on the judge's seat' (27:19).

In Matthew, it is while he is sitting in the judgement seat and talking to the crowd that Pilate's wife emerges and warns him, 'Don't have anything to do with that innocent man, for I have suffered a great deal today in a dream because of him.' (27:19)

Pilate's wife, who is unnamed here, does not appear in any of the other gospels. Since Matthew does not record any subsequent conversation between husband and wife, the reader gets the impression that the Prefect ignores her. It is possible, of course, that her apparent failure to influence his subsequent actions may be down to the fact that she never intervened in the first place, and that Matthew's whole brief episode of Pilate's wife is a later addition. In any case, it seems unlikely that a Roman lady of her class (if she was ever in Jerusalem, or if she ever existed at all) would have ventured out to a public place in the open air to try to interfere in a delicate case her husband was dealing with, in front of the Jewish officials and a potentially dangerous crowd. Since Pilate may only have taken up residence in Jerusalem at times when unrest was expected, it is also possible that he would have preferred to let her remain at Caesarea, where she could also have escaped by sea if the situation there suddenly became unstable. There is also another problem with this incident – the dream itself is not described, unlike many other dreams throughout the Bible.

Having ignored his wife's interpretation of her dream, Pilate goes on to offer the crowd the choice of Jesus or Barabbas again, and when they choose Barabbas and demand the crucifixion of Jesus, Pilate assents because he feels that otherwise some sort of riot might take place. This is subtly different from Mark, where Pilate agrees to this course of action *to please the people*. In the same verse in Matthew where Pilate agrees to the crucifixion of Jesus (27:24) the Prefect washes his hands: an iconic moment that does not occur in Mark.

This business of washing his hands – clearly a symbolic gesture intended to show that Pilate is denying all responsibility for what he is about to do – is immediately followed in Matthew by the crowd's assertion that *they* will take responsibility for Jesus' death: 'His blood is on us and on our children!' (27:25)

Again as in Mark, Joseph of Arimathea comes to Pilate to claim Jesus' body, but in Matthew the Jewish authorities insist that Pilate seal the tomb and post a guard at it. In the apocryphal Gospel of Peter, the provenance of which is disputed, Pilate is informed of wonders that are later seen at the tomb, and agrees to order his troops to keep quiet about them.

As if the differences between the treatment of Pilate in Matthew and Mark weren't surprising enough, the Gospel of Luke introduces more details. At last, at the start of Luke's third chapter, we learn Pilate's other name, 'Pontius'. Also in this chapter, we learn something about how Pilate's sphere of influence relates to nearby areas: to the north in Galilee, where Jesus was raised, Herod is tetrarch, and Herod's brother Philip is tetrarch of Iturea and Trachonitis, to the north and east of Galilee respectively. Luke even tells us that all this happened during the reign of the Roman emperor Tiberius (lived 42 BC-37 AD; emperor from 14 AD until his death).

At the start of Luke 13, some people come and tell Jesus that Pilate is responsible for killing a number of Galileans and mingling their blood with their sacrifices. This puzzling piece of news has no equivalent in the other gospels, and is not reflected in other histories of the time. It has been suggested that what happened was that Pilate was hunting down some men from Herod's province whom he, Pilate, considered to be criminals, and that he had them killed while they were sacrificing paschal lambs in the Jerusalem Temple, thus mingling human and animal blood. It is likely that this massacre was a recent event, since the paschal lambs were sacrificed at Passover, during the days of which festival Jesus' Passion is supposed to have happened. The men could be murdered while they were sacrificing because the paschal lambs did not have to be sacrificed by Temple priests – ordinary pilgrims, for instance from Galilee, could do the job. Although Luke 13 continues with a mention of eighteen men who were recently killed when a tower collapsed at Siloam in Jerusalem, it does not put a figure on the deaths in the Temple, if that is where Pilate had those other men killed.

Luke's treatment of Pilate's first encounter with Jesus starts at the beginning of Chapter 23, where the Jewish hierarchy give Pilate rather more reasons to condemn the Nazarene than are given in Mark or Matthew. According to them, Jesus is teaching sedition, instructing the people not to pay taxes to Caesar, and claiming to be 'Christ', meaning (according to the Jewish hierarchy) a king.

In Luke it seems that Pilate is supposed to be talking to the crowd and the Jewish hierarchy simultaneously, in the presence of Jesus, although Joel B. Green, in his 1997 commentary on Luke, suggests that 'the crowd' comprised only the Jewish authorities and their guards. Pilate asks his first question of Jesus: 'Are you the king of the Jews?'

(23:3) and Jesus replies as he does in Mark and Matthew. This brief questioning seems to be enough to make Pilate conclude that Jesus is innocent, and he gives the Jewish leaders the benefit of his opinion on the matter. They reply by accusing Jesus of stirring up the people; first in Galilee, then in Jerusalem.

The mention of Galilee makes Luke's version of Pilate ask if Jesus is a Galilean. When he hears that he is, the Prefect packs the Nazarene off to Herod Antipas, whom Luke has already told us is tetrarch of Galilee. Jesus' visit to Herod, who was nearby in Jerusalem at the time, is not mentioned in the other gospels, and Luke's account of it is brief: Herod, who has heard of this miracle-worker from his province, hopes Jesus will perform a miracle for him, but is disappointed. He asks Jesus many questions, but Jesus answers none of them. At last Herod's people ridicule Jesus, dress him up in a gorgeous robe, and send him back to Pilate. For some reason this episode cements a new friendship between Pilate and Herod, who had been enemies before. This, by the way, would seem to contradict the assertion in Acts 4:27 that Herod and Pilate met together to plan the downfall of Jesus.

Since, like Pilate's hand-washing and the dream of Pilate's wife, it only appears in one of the canonical gospels, doubt may legitimately be cast on the reality of Jesus' visit to Herod at this time. If, however, this is a later addition, then whoever added it did a reasonable job. As we will see, Pilate mentions Herod's role in the case during the next stage of the trial.

Back in front of 'the chief priests, the rulers and the people' (23:13) Luke's Pilate reiterates his opinion that Jesus is not guilty, and reminds everyone that Herod has found no fault in him either. Pilate then proposes a compromise: he will make Jesus the one prisoner who is released at Passover, but he will 'punish' him before he releases him; which in this context seems to suggest some form of corporal punishment. But the crowd still insist that they want Barabbas, identified by Luke as a seditious murderer. In response Pilate again offers them Jesus instead, but they cry out for Jesus' crucifixion. This exchange is repeated again, 'and their shouts prevailed' (23:23). Barabbas is released, and then Luke plunges straight into a narration of Jesus' crucifixion. Again, Pilate's last appearance in the gospel is when he allows Joseph of Arimathea to take Jesus' body away for burial.

The picture of Pilate that emerges from Mark, Matthew and Luke raises as many questions as it answers. The fundamental question is, what can we know for sure about Pilate, when so many details are not common to all the synoptic gospels, and when they even seem to contradict each other at several points. Key elements that are forever associated with Pilate's name only appear in one synoptic gospel: the Prefect only washes his hands in Matthew, though hundreds of paintings and manuscript illuminations show him doing this – in fact a bowl of water has become an attribute of Pilate in pictures, much as a wheel has become an attribute of Saint Catherine, and the presence of a lion helps us identify pictures of Saint Jerome.

Another element of the story that only appears in Matthew is the appearance of Pilate's wife, who warns him that he should have nothing to do with this innocent man called Jesus, about whom she has just dreamed a very troubling dream. A third episode that only appears in one of the gospels is Jesus' visit to Herod, which is only recounted in Luke.

More subtle differences between the gospels concern such factors as the exact charges brought against Jesus by the Jewish authorities, and Pilate's reason for consenting to release Barabbas to the Jews and order the crucifixion of Jesus, when he suspects that the Nazarene is quite innocent. Does he do this just to please the Jews, or does he fear that a riot might break out if he keeps Barabbas and releases Jesus?

The synoptic gospels agree that the Jewish authorities captured Jesus, then after some deliberation took him to Pilate to be tried and sentenced. The idea that Pilate believes that Jesus is innocent, but that the Prefect is prevailed upon to crucify him, is also common to Matthew, Mark and Luke, who all agree that Pilate's involvement in all this happened in Jerusalem during the Passover festival. All this is enough to allow the reader to attach some blame for Jesus' crucifixion to Pilate, but the brevity of all three accounts, and the way that they seem to contradict each other, tends to frustrate any attempt to form a reliable picture of Pilate. What was he like? What was he thinking? Why did he do and say what he did?

3. Pilate in the Gospel of John

In keeping with its status as the 'exceptional' gospel, the account of Pilate in the Gospel of John, which may have been written over seventy years after the crucifixion of Jesus, is radically different from the accounts in the synoptic gospels.

John's account of Pilate is much longer and more detailed than the equivalent accounts in the other gospels, partly because in John he is much more 'hands on' and involved in more stages of Jesus' Passion. In John's equivalent of Jesus' trial by Pilate, both Pilate and Jesus also have a lot more to say, and if we could trust John as a scrupulously factual account, then many of our questions about Pilate raised by reading the first three gospels would be answered by John.

John is much clearer about the setting of Pilate's first encounter with Jesus: he even gives us a rough time of day – very early in the morning. After the Nazarene has been questioned by the high priest Caiaphas, he is led to the praetorium. The Jews will not enter because to do so would make them ritually unclean: they want to avoid this defilement because it would exclude them from the Passover feast. It seems, however, that at certain points in this version Jesus is inside the 'praetorium' ('praitorion' in the original Greek), a word that is translated as 'hall of judgement' in the King James version, but identified as Pilate's palace in the

NIV.

Since the Jews will not enter his praetorium, Pilate has to go outside to speak to them, and he immediately asks them what crime Jesus is supposed to have committed. Their answer is so evasive that it hardly counts as an answer at all: 'If he were not a criminal,' they reply, 'we would not have handed him over to you' (18:30).

This exchange sets a trend that runs throughout Pilate's encounter with Jesus in the Gospel of John – the questions and answers reported here often do not quite seem to belong together – there is a kind of 'slippage' between them. This is reminiscent of frustrating conversations everyone has witnessed and participated in personally, where people talk at cross-purposes, or are so bound up in their own ideas that they are not willing or able to adapt their speech to the demands of the conversation. One characteristic of such fruitless, frustrating exchanges can be a high percentage of questions answered with further questions, something that is demonstrated very strikingly in John's account of Pilate's encounter with Jesus.

Sometimes the problem with such conversations is that one participant insists on returning to an earlier question, comment or statement, when the conversation has already moved on to something else: like the business of answering a question with a question, this can make participants in the conversation become disoriented. This also happens in John's account of Pilate and Jesus.

Responding to the evasive answer of the Jewish leaders, Pilate suggests that they take Jesus away and try him by their own laws – a reasonable suggestion, since they have just refused to tell Pilate what the prisoner is supposed to have done wrong. The Jewish leaders explain that they have no law whereby they can put Jesus to death – since Pilate can, by virtue of his office, hand out a death sentence, they have brought Jesus to him.

Although the people outside have not, in this version,

mentioned to Pilate that Jesus has claimed to be King of the Jews, Pilate goes back inside the praetorium and asks Jesus his familiar first question: 'Are you the king of the Jews?' (18:33)

Instead of answering briefly as he does in the other three gospels, John's version of Jesus responds with another question: 'Is that your own idea,' Jesus asks, 'or did others talk to you about me?' (18:34)

Pilate replies with two more questions, separated by a statement: 'Am I a Jew? [. . .] Your own people and chief priests handed you over to me. What is it you have done?' (18:35)

Jesus chooses this moment to answer Pilate's first question, this time with far more detail than appears in the synoptic gospels. As if trying to explain to the Prefect the difference between his, Pilate's, understanding of kingship and his own, which is based on the concept of the Messiah, Jesus tells the Prefect that his kingdom is not of this world: if it were, then he would have, in effect, a body-guard to defend him against the Jews. But Pilate seems not to be ready to understand this. He asks Jesus again if he is a king, and Jesus tells him that he was born for one purpose – to bear witness to the truth. Pilate answers again with a question – 'What is truth?' (18:38)

Jesus does not answer this question, and in this part of the Gospel of John the question just seems to hang there, mysterious and suggestive. Why did Pilate ask it? Did he expect an answer? Was he wanting to start a debate, in the style of the Greek philosophers? Was he actually inviting Jesus to favour him with his essential message?

After this, Pilate goes outside again to tell the Jewish authorities that he can find no fault in Jesus, and to suggest that he make this King of the Jews the prisoner he will release as per the Passover custom. In reply, they say that they want Barabbas instead.

In the synoptic gospels, Pilate hands Jesus over to his

soldiers to receive physical punishment after his trial before the Prefect, but in John, Pilate himself scourges Jesus, or orders him to be scourged, in the middle of his encounter with the Nazarene, the Jewish authorities and the crowd. The context suggests that this all happened inside the praetorium, while the crowd waited outside. As in Matthew and Mark, the crown of thorns is put on Jesus' head; and he is given a purple robe, intended to mock his alleged royal aspirations.

Pilate then returns to the crowd outside and announces that he intends to show them Jesus, in whom he can find no fault. Jesus is then brought out from wherever he has been inside the praetorium, and shown to the people.

It seems that John has brought the narrative elements of the crown of thorns, the scourging and the mocking robe forward to an earlier part of the narrative, and also allowed his Pilate to attempt to put into action his plan to release Jesus, having first punished him. But the crowd do not let the Prefect follow this plan through.

It is tempting to speculate on how Pilate thought the crowd would react to the sight of the scourged, bleeding figure who is shown to them. Did he hope that the people would feel sorry for Jesus, decide that he had suffered enough, and claim him as the prisoner whom they wanted released at Passover?

It may be that some of the *people* were cowed by the sight of Jesus in this state, and would have liked to have seen him released instead of Barabbas; but John tells us that *the chief priests and their officials* cried out for Jesus' crucifixion. Now Pilate tells them that they should take Jesus away and crucify him themselves (though this form of execution was Roman and not Jewish in character) and again we have a reply that is not a direct response to a question or demand – the officials tell Pilate that they have a law that says Jesus must die because he has claimed to be the Son of God. This revelation makes Pilate 'more afraid' (19:8).

31

There is 'slippage' between Pilate's suggestion and the officials' response here because a more logical reply would have been for them to say something like, 'We cannot crucify him: that is not a custom of ours; but we want you to crucify him. By our laws, he is worthy of death because he claims to be the Son of God.'

By this time it seems that Jesus has been led back into the praetorium again: did Pilate have him removed as soon as it became clear that the ploy of showing him to the people had not worked; or did he fear that the people would pull him down and 'lynch' him; and so had him taken back inside where he would be safer, since none of the Jews wanted to make themselves ritually unclean by entering the place?

Rushing back into the praetorium, Pilate asks Jesus where he is from, but gets no reply. Again, there seems to be some slippage between Pilate's question and what has gone before: at this point, shouldn't the Prefect be asking Jesus not where he comes from, but whether he thinks of himself as the Son of God?

When Jesus offers no reply, Pilate tries to remind him that he, Pilate, is the man who has the power to either release him or have him crucified. Jesus then points out that the Prefect has no power except what is granted him by God, and that the man who handed him, Jesus, over to Pilate is more guilty than Pilate himself (presumably Jesus is referring to Judas here).

Pilate's response to being told that he is a mere puppet of the Almighty is to go outside again and continue to petition for Jesus' release. But 'the Jews', which here seems to mean both the officials and the people, now warn Pilate that if he allows a man who claims to be a king to go free, then he is no friend of Caesar (meaning the emperor Tiberius). In response to this, Pilate has Jesus brought out, and himself sits down in the judgement seat. He introduces Jesus to the people as their king, and asks them if he should crucify such a figure, but the people continue to cry out for his crucifixion, while the Jewish officials claim that they have 'no king but Caesar' (19:15).

From the judgement seat Pilate at last sentences Jesus to crucifixion, and the Nazarene is led away; but the Prefect's involvement does not end there or with the handing over of the body to Joseph of Arimathea. John tells us that Pilate personally made, or had made, the sign that was put on Jesus' cross, saying in Hebrew, Latin and Greek that Jesus was the King of the Jews (the NIV substitutes 'Aramaic' for Hebrew here). The Jews themselves object to the wording of this sign, saying that the words should be changed to 'I am the King of the Jews', but Pilate does not agree to the change.

Later, when 'the Jews' want to speed up the deaths of Jesus and the two men crucified with him, because it is still the eve of Passover, Pilate gives them permission to break their legs; but Jesus is found to be dead already. When Pilate allows Joseph of Arimathea to take down Jesus' body, the Prefect's role in John's Passion narrative at last comes to an end.

As we have seen, John's account of Pilate's contact with Jesus is very specific about setting, carefully telling us whether certain exchanges happen inside or outside the praetorium. The way that Pilate feels compelled to shuttle between the inside and the outside could almost become comic in a dramatic presentation of the scene. John is also specific about the location of the judgement seat Pilate assumes before passing sentence: this is at a place called The Pavement, known as Gabbatha in Hebrew, a hill on which part of Jerusalem's Antonia fortress had been built by Herod the Great. John also tells us that Jesus' 'trial' before Pilate lasts from very early in the morning until noon (or 'the sixth hour'). We might assume that noon in the open air in Jerusalem, when the trial finally ended, would be so hot and sunny that Pilate would be keen to put an end to it and get into some cool shade. It is likely, however, that the noon temperature at this time of year would not have been much hotter than a comfortable eighteen centigrade (around sixty-five Fahrenheit).

If we take 'very early' to be around dawn on this spring day, then the whole procedure as reported by John would have taken an astonishing six hours. If John is right about his times, then we must assume that many of the exchanges he records were even longer than he set down, and that there were periods of waiting around, when nothing much was happening – did Pilate keep the Jewish officials waiting before he first appeared, for instance?

It is also implied that some exchanges happened 'off camera' that John did not report in detail. Did one or more of the Jewish officials harangue the crowd at length, perhaps more than once, to remind them to demand the crucifixion of Jesus, and to give them reasons for doing so?

Although John's account of Pilate's time with Jesus is extremely detailed, crossing from one chapter into another and stretching over fifty verses, there is no record of Pilate's iconic hand-washing here. Pilate's wife is also not mentioned, and Jesus is not sent to Herod; though the business of putting a purple cloak on the Nazarene resembles the way Herod's men put a fine cloak on Jesus, to mock him.

Whereas in Mark in particular we get the idea that Pilate wants to dispense with the whole business of Jesus as quickly as possible, having first made some token attempts to probe into his case, John's Pilate, a much more active, even frenetic, figure, seems to fight hard during several hours to find a way to save Jesus from the cross. At last, he places himself in the judgement seat.

The misunderstandings, and what I have called the 'slippages' between questions and answers in John are to some extent present in the other gospels' treatments of Pilate's interactions with the Jewish authorities, the people and Jesus himself. These read like the familiar symptoms of culture-clash, a phenomenon that can often be observed when people from one culture try to interact with those from a distinct culture with which they are unfamiliar. These problems often go far beyond language differences, and can still happen when there is a useful *lingua franca* that the representatives of the contrasting cultures can use.

A lot of the misunderstanding reflected in the gospels' treatment of Pilate's role centres on the word 'Messiah'. As we have seen, the Jewish conception of the Messiah in Jesus' time was much more regal than the outwardly humble figure Jesus must have cut, especially in the wealthy city of Jerusalem. While Jesus and some of his fellow Jews might have disagreed about what the Messiah was meant to be like, there is evidence in the gospels that Pilate might have been quite unable to grasp this concept adequately; a concept which would only find its way into his mother tongue later, when Latin-speaking Romans began to be baptised as Christians.

Sometimes Pilate seems to think of Jesus' messianic aspirations as part of an attempt by the Nazarene to make himself a local king; but it is unlikely that the Prefect thought of kingship as an exclusively secular role. The emperor of Rome, the nearest thing to a king that the Prefect would have learned about back in Italy, had a religious role as high pontiff of the state religion, and the first emperor, Augustus, had been deified upon death. There was a lively cult of this divine emperor by the time Pilate was appointed to the governorship of Judea by Augustus' successor Tiberius, and, as we shall see, Pilate personally seemed to think that worship of, or at least reverence for, a living emperor was no bad thing.

Given his understanding of how divinity and earthly rule could combine in the person of a Roman emperor, it may be that Pilate (and indeed many of the Jews in Jerusalem at this time) could not conceive of a Messiah whose kingdom was

35

not of this world, a claim Jesus makes about the character of his kingdom in John's version of events.

Even if Jesus was seen not as a king but a prophet of Israel, in the style of the Old Testament prophets, then the high priests, who must have known their Jewish history, would also have seen him as a threat to their power. Some of those old prophets, such as Amos, took a dim view of some of the goings-on of the priests of their own times. Quoting God himself, Amos says:

I hate, I despise your religious festivals;
your assemblies are a stench to me.
Even though you bring me burnt offerings and grain offerings,
I will not accept them.
Though you bring choice fellowship offerings,
I will have no regard for them.

(Amos 5:21-22)

It would seem from the Gospel of Matthew that the idea that Jesus might be an Old Testament prophet was current among at least some of Jesus' contemporaries. When Jesus asks his disciples who people say the Son of Man is, they reply 'Some say John the Baptist; others say Elijah; and still others, Jeremiah or one of the prophets' (Mt 16:14).

4. Other Voices

Despite the evidence to be found in the New Testament and elsewhere, there are still scholars who believe that Jesus did not exist, or, if he did, had very little to do with what they see as the mythological figure of Jesus Christ as he is known to Christians. In his 2012 book *Jesus and His World*, Craig A. Evans focuses on the ideas of one of these sceptics, the Canadian priest Tom Harpur, author of *The Pagan Christ* (2004). Among other arguments, Harpur cites the similarities between the biographies of other sacred beings, including the Egyptian god Horus, the Persian Mithras, and Buddha, and the story of Christ, to justify his idea that Jesus was not a real man, but a figment of somebody's imagination. Evidently, part of Craig Evans' motivation for writing his book, which is subtitled *The Archaeological Evidence*, was to call theories such as Harpur's into question.

Though 'minimalists' such as Harpur, who died in 2017, may believe that it is possible to disprove the existence of Jesus, it is perhaps rather more difficult to deny or disprove the existence of Pontius Pilate, whose role in the crucifixion of Jesus is also affirmed in the creeds regularly recited in Christian churches. As a prefect of Judea who is allotted no supernatural powers in the gospels, it is hard to argue that Pilate is some mythological or imaginary being whom the early Christians sought to turn into a historical character.

An ancient text that cannot be used as evidence that Pilate never existed, but does erase Pontius Pilate from its account of the story of Jesus' trial, can be found in the Babylonian Talmud, a vast compendium of Jewish Rabbinical writings on many subjects that probably reached its final form around 700 AD. The Babylonian Talmud is divided into some sixty so-called 'tractates', one of these being Tractate Sanhedrin, which deals with aspects of law and justice. Sanhedrin 43a discusses the legal use of heralds to spread information about a case at law to the people. The part of Tractate Sanhedrin that mentions Jesus implies that Jesus (called 'Yeshu', short for 'Yeshua', here) was tried by a Jewish court without any interference from the Roman authorities. Here we also learn that Yeshu was hanged on the eve of Passover, having first perhaps been stoned, partly because nobody would come forward to defend him. The heralds that are the subject of this tractate were apparently used to call on anyone who wanted to to defend Yeshu in court: nobody stepped forward. In this part of the Talmud, Yeshu is described as deserving of his fate, and not deserving of a legal defence, because he was a sorcerer and a *mesith*, meaning an enticer, who tried to lead his followers away from the true Jewish path.

While the Talmud removes Pilate and the Romans from the trial of Jesus altogether, the apocryphal Gospel of Peter places Pilate at the trial, but minimises his guilt. Here, once the Prefect has washed his hands and noticed that the representatives of the Jewish authorities will not do so, he leaves. Then Herod Antipas, who is present at the trial in this version, sentences Jesus to death.

Although a gospel of Peter is mentioned in early texts, it was thought to have been lost until the French archaeologist Urbain Bouriant discovered a fragment of it 1886 in the Egyptian city of Akhmim, buried with a monk and preserved because of the dry conditions characteristic of Egypt. Although the fragment itself dates from the eighth or ninth centuries, the provenance of the actual text is disputed.

Like that of Jesus (or Yeshu), Pilate's historical existence can be confirmed by reference to near-contemporary sources, outside of the New Testament, that mention him. An ancient author who gives an account of Pilate but not of Jesus is Philo of Alexandria. Philo's dates are not known with any exactitude, but it is known that he was an older contemporary of Jesus. Also known as Philo Judeaus, he was a Jewish philosopher from the Egyptian city of Alexandria, which was then part of the Roman empire and had a large population of Jews and a thriving intellectual life.

The work by Philo that includes Pontius Pilate is the *Embassy to Gaius,* his description of a diplomatic mission to Rome that he led, which was intended to present some grievances of the Alexandrian Jews to Gaius, the Roman emperor who is often known by his childhood nick-name, Caligula. The Alexandrian Jews wanted to petition Caligula about their treatment at the hands of some of the riotous Greeks of Alexandria, and also about the anti-Semitic policies of the prefect Aulus Avilius Flaccus, who insisted on putting statues of the emperor in Alexandrian synagogues; a terrible offence to the Jewish prohibition on graven images.

In his book *The Twelve Caesars*, the Roman historian Suetonius offers his opinion that Caligula was quite mad, and presents plenty of evidence to prove it. This is the emperor who is supposed to have given his favourite horse a marble stable with an ivory manger, in a house staffed by human servants. He is also supposed to have slept with all three of his sisters, and even set up a brothel in the royal palace in an attempt to raise money. From the point of view of pious Pagan Romans, Caligula's belief that he had become a god while he was still alive was perhaps the worst symptom of his madness. He would stand in a temple, like the statue of a god, to receive sacrifices personally; and when Philo's Jewish embassy met him, complained to them that though they might have sacrificed *for him* to their

Jewish God, they had not sacrificed *to him directly*, as a god in his own right.

Much of Philo's *Embassy to Gaius* is taken up with the alarming business of Caligula ordering that a gorgeous gold-plated statue of himself as the Roman god Jupiter should be set up in the holy of holies of the Temple at Jerusalem. This was evidently regarded as much worse than any attempt to try such a thing in a provincial synagogue. In his *Embassy*, Philo has Caligula's Jewish friend King Herod Agrippa, a grandson of Herod the Great, send the emperor a lengthy letter in which he explains why the erection of such a statue was unthinkable to the Jewish nation; and arguing that Caligula's predecessors, the emperor Tiberius, and Augustus himself, would never have contemplated such a thing.

In his letter, Herod does not mention Tiberius's brutal expulsion of all Jews from Rome in 19 AD, and instead recalls the time when the prefect of Judea, Pontius Pilate, set up some gilded shields or plaques in his house in Jerusalem, with inscriptions on them about himself and his imperial master Tiberius. This, says Herod, was done deliberately to offend the Jews, as well as to honour Tiberius.

When the Jews complained, Herod reminds Caligula, Tiberius ordered Pilate to remove the plaques to the coastal city of Caesarea. In his letter, Herod points out to Caligula that both the Jews and the emperor Tiberius objected to these plaques, although there were no images on them such as would have offended the Jews with their prohibition of graven images. And they had not even been put on public display, only hung up indoors in one of Pilate's own palaces, the re-purposed palace of Herod the Great in Jerusalem.

As if to bring home to Caligula that to offend the Jews in this way is monstrous, Herod mentions Pilate's general wickedness, though without giving any more specific examples. According to him, Pilate was ferocious, inflexible, merciless, obstinate, corrupt, insolent, insulting, cruel and guilty of 'rapine', 'ferocious passions', 'continual murders of people untried and uncondemned' and 'never-ending, and gratuitous, and most grievous inhumanity'.

Philo's embassy to Caligula, and that emperor's insane plan to put his statue in the Jerusalem Temple, are also mentioned in the *Jewish Antiquities*, the history of the Jews written by the Jewish historian Josephus (37-100 AD). Josephus does not mention the shields or plaques Pilate used to decorate Herod's old palace, which the Prefect was using as his base in Jerusalem, but he does give accounts of a far greater crime committed by Pilate against Jewish sensibilities.

In both his *Jewish Antiquities* and his *Jewish War*, Josephus relates how, under cover of night, Pilate had his soldiers bring ensigns or *signa* into the city, which bore images of the emperor Tiberius. In the *Jewish Antiquities*, Josephus includes the information that the soldiers with the *signa* had been transferred from Caesarea to winter in Jerusalem. The historian adds that all the previous Roman prefects of Judea had had their soldiers carry only standards without graven images.

As day dawned, the Jews of Jerusalem were horrified to see what Pilate had done, which to their minds transgressed the rejection of graven images that was at the heart of their faith, enshrined in the second commandment:

You shall not make for yourself an image in the form of anything in heaven above or on the earth beneath or in the waters below. You shall not bow down to them or worship them; for I, the Lord your God, am a jealous God, punishing the children for the sin of the parents to the third and fourth generation of those who hate me, but showing love to a thousand generations of those who love me and keep my commandments.

Where the ten commandments appear in Exodus 20, the

second commandment can seem like an extension of the first: 'You shall have no other gods before me'. For the Jews of Jerusalem that morning, Pilate's transgression may have seemed to violate at least two commandments – the first against graven images and the second against worshipping gods other than Jehovah. Although technically the Roman emperors were not deified until after death, Tiberius's relationship to the deified Augustus made him something of a god-like figure during life, and, as we shall see, Pilate may have thought of him as a person worthy of veneration if not actual worship while he still lived and reigned.

In her exhaustive book on Pilate, Ann Wroe suggests that he brought the offending standards into Jerusalem near the start of his time as prefect, and that the gesture showed his youth and inexperience. We may also read this action as another attempt to deliberately annoy the Jews, which Philo offers as part of Pilate's motivation for putting up the controversial plaques. Josephus is convinced that the intrusion of the offending standards into the heart of the holy city of Jerusalem was part of Pilate's plan to destroy the Jewish religion.

Josephus tells us is that crowds of people went to complain to Pilate about the standards, at Caesarea, his base on the coast, over seventy miles to the north and west of Jerusalem. The fact that Pilate was at Caesarea suggests either that the Prefect had not been with the soldiers and the standards when they entered Jerusalem at night, preferring to stay at Caesarea, or that he had hot-footed it back to Caesarea very soon after the standards had been installed.

In any case, the fact that Pilate was at Caesarea when 'multitudes' of the locals came there to petition him suggests that only a proportion of the soldiers under his command can have been transferred to Jerusalem at this time: he would have needed a considerable number to protect him at Caesarea.

For five days the Jews petitioned Pilate to remove the

offending standards, but he resisted them, partly because to remove them (or perhaps the offending parts of them) would have been an offence to the emperor. By the sixth day, Pilate had grown tired of the protests, and decided to set up an ambush for the protestors.

He made a show of appearing in the judgement seat at Caesarea, which was presumably the local version of the judgement seat in Jerusalem from which the Gospel of John has Pilate sentence Jesus. Things were arranged so that as the protestors assembled around Pilate's seat, they could not see that he had a number of armed soldiers concealed and ready to pounce on them at a pre-arranged signal.

When the signal was given, the soldiers showed themselves, and Pilate threatened that if the crowd did not disperse immediately and stop pestering him, he would have the soldiers massacre them all. This plan did not turn out as Pilate probably hoped. The protestors hurled themselves to the ground, showed their bare necks and declared that they would rather die than continue to see their laws transgressed. Josephus tells us that Pilate was deeply impressed by this, and decided to have the offending standards moved back to Caesarea – the place where the notorious plaques also ended up.

Straight after his account of the *signa* incident in the *Jewish Antiquities*, Josephus tells us about Pilate's next problem, which should not have been a problem at all, but something that might have made him the most popular Roman prefect of Judea in history. This was a scheme to build an aqueduct to bring a fresh water supply to Jerusalem, a city where water could be in short supply, and where the citizens often relied on water stored in tanks and cisterns.

But to fund this worthwhile scheme, Pilate drew on the sacred 'corban' money of the Temple, and so 'tens of thousands' of offended locals turned out to try to persuade the Prefect to abandon the project. This time, Josephus does not specify where the protest took place, but he makes it clear that Pilate personally confronted the protestors again, this time demanding that they disperse. When they refused to budge, and moreover began to abuse him, Pilate gave a pre-arranged signal, and the soldiers whom he had placed in the crowd, armed with daggers and disguised as locals, began to strike out.

Josephus tells us that the disguised soldiers were much more violent that Pilate had intended, killing both 'tumultuous' protestors and innocent bystanders indiscriminately. As the protestors were unarmed and taken by surprise, there was great panic and loss of life, and many of those who managed to run away were wounded.

The account of Pilate's tainted aqueduct is followed in the *Jewish Antiquities* by Josephus's most important reference to Jesus Christ, which is worth inserting here in full:

Now there was about this time Jesus, a wise man, if it be lawful to call him a man; for he was a doer of wonderful works, a teacher of such men as receive the truth with pleasure. He drew over to him both many of the Jews and many of the Gentiles. He was [the] Christ. And when Pilate, at the suggestion of the principal men amongst us, had condemned him to the cross, those that loved him at the first did not forsake him; for he appeared to them alive again the third day; as the divine prophets had foretold these and ten thousand other wonderful things concerning him. And the tribe of Christians, so named from him, are not extinct at this day.

(Josephus, Jewish Antiquities 18:63, trans. Whiston)

Scholars have long suspected that all or some of this famous passage was added later by a Christian editor: certainly New Testament minimalists such as Tom Harpur would assert that none of it is genuine. If all of it is fake, then at least the forger chose a good place to insert his bogus passage – right at the end of a section on the crimes of Pontius Pilate.

The short account of Jesus in the *Annals* of the Roman historian Tacitus is along much the same lines as Josephus's version, though it has a higher reputation for genuineness. It also refers to Pilate, and is part of Tacitus's description of the aftermath of a terrible fire that swept through Rome in 64 AD:

[The Emperor] Nero fastened the guilt and inflicted the most exquisite tortures on a class hated for their abominations, called Christians by the populace. Christus, from whom the name had its origin, suffered the extreme penalty during the reign of Tiberius at the hands of one of our procurators, Pontius Pilatus, and a most mischievous superstition, thus checked for the moment, again broke out not only in Judea, the first source of the evil, but even in Rome, where all things hideous and shameful from every part of the world find their centre and become popular. Accordingly, an arrest was first made of all who pleaded guilty; then, upon their information, an immense multitude was convicted, not so much of the crime of firing the city, as of hatred against mankind.

(Tacitus, *Annals* 15:44, trans. Church & Brodribb)

After a description of the events leading up to the near-simultaneous expulsion of the Jews and of the cult of the Egyptian goddess Isis from Rome in 19 AD by the emperor Tiberius, Josephus gives an account of Pilate's final atrocity in Judea, which did not involve the Jews, but rather the separate ethnic and religious group known in English as the Samaritans.

The details of what we might call the Tirathaba incident

are unclear, but it seems that an unnamed con-man persuaded a large number of Samaritans to arm themselves and assemble at a village called Tirathaba.

The plan was that they would all set out together and climb Gerizzim, the sacred mountain of the Samaritans, where the con-man claimed he would unearth for them some sacred vessels Moses had buried there. For some reason Pilate sent troops to attack these pilgrims, and there was another massacre. The Samaritans complained to Lucius Vitellius, the Roman ruler of Syria, who replaced Pilate with a man called Marcellus and sent him back to Rome. By the time Pilate reached the eternal city, however, the emperor Tiberius was dead.

The idea of Pilate we get from contemporary or near-contemporary references from beyond the New Testament is by no means as positive as the impression created by the gospels, especially the Gospel of John. Philo's description of him as ferocious, obstinate and cruel would seem to be justified from what we learn of his actions from Philo and Josephus: the exception might be his theoretically laudable aqueduct scheme, which was however tainted by some other likely aspects of his personality – his ignorance, insensitivity and impatience.

The Pilate of John's Gospel is a sensitive, concerned soul by contrast to the Pilate who sent his assassins in amongst a crowd of unarmed protestors, or slaughtered Samaritan pilgrims. John's Pilate seems to condemn Jesus to death only with the greatest reluctance, having first rushed back and forth for hours, trying to understand every aspect of the case, and repeatedly offering to save Jesus from the cross. Eventually, Pilate even insists on describing Jesus as the King of the Jews on the famous placard that was fixed to his cross, resisting any change to the wording, suggesting that perhaps he himself had become convinced of Jesus' importance.

5. Later Voices

With Pilate's dismissal and replacement at the hands of Vitellius, and his return to Rome to find Tiberius dead, the most famous Roman prefect of Judea effectively steps out of the spotlight of history. We know nothing about his later life with anything like even the partial certainty we can feel about at least the outline of the New Testament story, and some of the details from Philo, Josephus and Tacitus.

But the character of Pilate captured the imagination of Christian readers, and it seems that a number of Christian writers set about hauling him out of the shadowy wings into the spotlight again, by any means possible.

Drawing on earlier traditions and authors, including the third century African Tertullian, Eusebius of Caesarea, who probably died in his eighties around 340 AD, tells us that as part of his duties as a prefect Pilate informed the emperor Tiberius about the life, death, resurrection and ascension of Jesus. Tiberius was so impressed that he tried to persuade the Roman senate to add Jesus to the pantheon of Roman gods, but the senate refused to do so. Eusebius adds that Pilate's account of Jesus also caused the emperor to refuse to persecute the Christians, and to forbid anyone else to do so.

Eusebius also tells us that Pilate experienced such misfortune under the next emperor, Caligula, that he felt compelled to kill himself. Eusebius sees this as an example of divine vengeance, which the historian also believed overtook the Jewish nation during the decades following what Eusebius sees as their betrayal of Jesus.

It is striking that Eusebius, who claims that earlier Greek historians recorded Pilate's suicide, does not attribute Pilate's act to unbearable remorse, which, it is implied in the New Testament, was Judas's reason for hanging himself.

A great deal of extra information about Pilate is also contained in an apocryphal text called the Gospel of Nicodemus, or the Acts of Pilate. This survives in several different versions, and was supposedly translated into Greek from a Hebrew record set down by Nicodemus, a follower of Jesus mentioned in the New Testament Book of Acts. Some of the material on Pilate that is found here is also found in the apocryphal Acts of Peter and Paul.

In the first Greek version of Nicodemus, we learn that when the Jewish authorities accused Jesus of casting out demons in the name of 'Beelzebul prince of the demons', Pilate offered his opinion, that Jesus was actually doing this in the name of Aesculapius, the Roman god of medicine (quotations from the Gospel of Nicodemus are from Volume VIII of *The Anti-Nicene Fathers* edited by Roberts and Donaldson).

When Pilate sends a messenger out to fetch Jesus to the place where he is consulting with the Jewish authorities, the messenger recognises Jesus: he witnessed his triumphal entry into Jerusalem on what we now call Palm Sunday, and, it is implied, was immediately convinced that he was worthy of reverence. The messenger therefore takes off his own cloak and lays it down for Jesus to walk on as he enters Pilate's presence.

As Jesus comes in, a miracle happens: two sets of Roman military standards that are being held up by standard-bearers in the place bend themselves down to do Jesus reverence. Presumably, these were standards like the ones Pilate had smuggled into Jerusalem by night, though perhaps without the iconography that proved to be so offensive to the Jewish locals.

Seeing the miracle of the bowing standards, the Jewish authorities accuse the standard-bearers of dipping them themselves, but they protest that they are Pagan Greeks and would never do so. 'The tops bent down of their own accord, and adored him,' they protest.

And so Pilate tries an experiment. He gets the Jews present to detail six strong men to hold each standard firm, and asks Jesus to go out and come in again. If the standards do not bow now, Pilate assures the original standard-bearers, I will have you both beheaded. But of course the standards do bow.

Also in Nicodemus, the wife of Pilate enters and warns him about Jesus as she does in Matthew, but here, when she has gone out again, Pilate reminds the Jewish authorities that his wife is a devotee of their religion. Repeating an accusation that is reminiscent of the account of Jesus' trial in Tractate Sanhedrin of the Babylonian Talmud, the Jewish authorities explain Pilate's wife's dream by saying that Jesus is a sorcerer, and put the dream into her head.

Some of the Jews present then accuse Jesus of being illegitimate, of performing miracles on the Sabbath and causing the massacre of the innocents (reported in Matthew 2:16-18). There then follows an argument about Jesus' legitimacy or otherwise, with Caiaphas and Annas (the High Priest and his influential father-in-law) arguing that Jesus was indeed 'born of fornication'; and that the minority present who say he was not are not really Jews at all, but only Greeks who have converted to Judaism.

Much else in the Gospel of Nicodemus's account is similar to what can be read in the canonical gospels and elsewhere in the New Testament, except that here Pilate's mysterious question 'What is truth?' gets an answer. 'Truth is from heaven,' Jesus says. When Pilate asks if truth is to be found on earth, Jesus adds 'Thou seest how those who speak the truth are judged by those that have the power upon earth'.

Another difference between the Gospel of Nicodemus and the canonical accounts of Jesus' trial before Pilate is that in this very long account some of the Jews present argue for the release of Jesus, and even weep openly when it starts to look as if the Nazarene will indeed be executed. Nicodemus himself also speaks in Jesus' defence, in terms reminiscent of Gamaliel's defence of the Christian apostles in Acts 5:39: 'If the miracles which he does are of God, they will stand;' says Nicodemus, 'but if man, they will come to nothing'.

There then follow accounts of some of the miracles of Jesus, some from the mouths of the beneficiaries themselves, who have come to Jesus' trial before Pilate as witnesses to tell their stories. These include a blind man whose sight was miraculously restored. But still some of the Jews cry out for Jesus' death, and Pilate gives them an impromptu and surprising lesson in their own history, to show them how they are characteristically rebellious and ungrateful:

Your God led you out of the land of Egypt from bitter slavery, and brought you safe through the sea as through dry land, and in the desert fed you with manna, and gave you quails, and quenched your thirst with water from a rock, and gave you a law; and in all these things you provoked your God to anger, and sought a molten calf. And you exasperated your God, and He sought to slay you. And Moses prayed for you, and you were not put to death.

In the Gospel of Nicodemus, Pilate, whose anger turns to fear at this point, is only driven to the symbolic washing of his hands when the accusation that Jesus caused the massacre of the innocents is repeated.

The Gospel of Nicodemus or Acts of Pilate falls into two distinct parts. After the gospel's account of the Passion with its novel 'take' on Jesus' trial before Pilate, there is a detailed account of Jesus' descent into hell, also known as the harrowing of hell. Like Pilate's role in the Passion narrative, the descent into hell is mentioned in Christian creeds; although there is scant evidence for it in the New Testament. The idea is that while Jesus' body was lying dead in Joseph of Arimathea's tomb, awaiting resurrection, his soul descended into hell, freed all the dead who had been imprisoned there since the time of Adam (including Adam himself) and allowed the righteous among the dead to reach heaven.

In Nicodemus' version of the harrowing of hell, the Jewish authorities and some of Jesus' followers hear about the recent upheavals in Hades from three men who have returned from the dead; Simeon and his two sons. Simeon was the old man who greeted Joseph, Mary and Jesus when they first entered the Jerusalem Temple together (Lk 2:25-35). The idea that these men have left their sepulchres and resumed their lives again is probably based on a hint to be found in Matthew's account of the death of Jesus:

At that moment the curtain of the temple was torn in two from top to bottom. The earth shook, the rocks split and the tombs broke open. The bodies of many holy people who had died were raised to life. They came out of the tombs after Jesus' resurrection and went into the holy city and appeared to many people.

(Mt 27:51-53)

In the Gospel of Nicodemus, we learn that even more of the righteous dead return to life at the time of Jesus' resurrection.

In some versions of Nicodemus, Pilate is told about these resurrections and the harrowing of hell, and decides to investigate by ordering a closed meeting with the Jewish authorities inside the Temple itself. At this meeting, the Jews admit that Jesus must be the Messiah, not only because of the miraculous signs he has performed, but also because of ancient prophecies to be found in their Jewish holy books. Pilate makes sure all of this is carefully recorded in his official files, and sends a letter to the emperor (here called Claudius, the 'King of Rome': Tiberius was from the Claudian family) giving a true account of events.

Pilate's letter to 'Claudius' is not the only letter to remain extant among the documents associated with the Gospel of Nicodemus. There are at least two Greek versions of Pilate's report about Jesus sent to 'August Caesar'. Here we learn that Pilate actually witnessed some of the events surrounding the harrowing of hell in Jerusalem, and did not just hear about them at second or third hand. He saw many of the dead walking again, witnessed shining angelic creatures, and even saw a great chasm that appeared and swallowed up a number of people.

In another apocryphal document called The Giving Up of Pontius Pilate, we see the Emperor Tiberius's response to this information about Jesus. Because of the reports he has received, the Emperor decides that Jesus must have been greater than all the Roman gods, and he summons Pilate back to Rome to explain himself. A bizarre trial of Pilate in front of Tiberius and the whole senate then takes place, in a Roman temple to all the gods. When the name of Jesus is mentioned at this gathering, all the statues of the gods fall down and are shattered. After further questioning of Pilate, Tiberius becomes even more convinced of the holiness of Jesus, has Pilate beheaded, and unleashes terrible vengeance on the Jews. But Pilate's head is received by an angel, a voice from heaven says that he is forever blessed, and his wife dies the death of a saint at the same time.

In another apocryphal account, called the Death of Pilate, we learn that Tiberius became dangerously ill, heard of a miraculous healer called Jesus, and sent a messenger to Pilate with orders to bring the miracle-worker to Rome. The messenger, Volusianus, learned from Pilate that Jesus was already dead, but luckily bumped into Saint Veronica elsewhere in Jerusalem.

According to Christian legend, Veronica gave Jesus a cloth to wipe his face when he was on his way to the cross. When the saint got the cloth back, there was a picture of Jesus on it. In The Death of Pilate, her story is different – she was carrying some canvas on which she wanted someone to paint a portrait of Jesus, but Jesus himself caused his own image to appear on the canvas.

Veronica explains to Volusianus that if the ailing emperor touches this canvas, he will be restored to health. Since the saint will not be parted from her picture, Veronica and the imperial messenger proceed to Rome together.

When Tiberius is cured by the picture, he becomes quite certain about the greatness of Jesus, and also about the wickedness of Pilate. He summons Pilate to Rome, but because Pilate is wearing a piece of clothing that had once belonged to Jesus, Tiberius cannot speak harshly to him, or pass sentence on him. Only when Pilate removes Jesus' garment can Tiberius order him to be locked up. Eventually, Pilate is sentenced to a 'most disgraceful death' and stabs himself to death to avoid it. This is another story of Pilate's suicide that does not attribute the act to overpowering guilt and remorse. Pilate's body is thrown into the River Tiber, but has to be dragged out again because it is haunted by demons that disturb the locals. The same thing happens in the River Rhone at Vienne, and eventually Pilate is buried among the mountains near Lausanne (not Lucerne, as some stories relate).

The many apocryphal texts that include information about Pontius Pilate, just some of which are described above, can make for entertaining (if surreal) reading, and some cast interesting side-lights on Pilate as a character; but scholars generally agree that they were all written down far too late to be really authoritative. The Gospel of Nicodemus is not usually placed at any time earlier than over three hundred years after the death of Jesus, and even Eusebius belongs to the fourth century.

It may be that aspects of these texts that cannot be found in the canonical New Testament date from closer to the time of Jesus, but in many cases it seems that some later author has taken a small hint from the gospels, for instance, and blown that up into a spectacular fable.

There is a tendency in some of these later texts, particularly The Giving Up of Pontius Pilate, to paint Pilate as a sympathetic, even saintly figure, while simultaneously blaming the Jews for the death of Jesus. 'They made me do it,' Pilate seems to be saying, and we are supposed to believe him. Eusebius in particular goes to great lengths to prove that the Jews' guilt over the death of Jesus caused them to have nothing but bad luck later on: the destruction of the Jerusalem Temple by the Romans in 70 AD just served them right.

The Anti-Semitism implied in this approach can be traced back to the Gospel of John, if not earlier. Here Pilate is shown to be desperate to save Jesus, but the Jews won't have it; and even Jesus, a Jew himself, blames them. In the later apocryphal texts, the warm light that sometimes shines on the figure of Pilate, leaving the Jews in the cold, deep shade, also shines on the Emperor Tiberius, who is shown to be wise and just. This sits uncomfortably with what we know about the life of this emperor, who was a truly nightmarish boss, having many of his subjects executed for no sane reason, leaving the levers of power in the hands of the ruthless, Jew-hating Sejanus, and molesting children at his lavishly-appointed estate on Capri.

Although devoted modern readers of the standard Christian bibles may remain ignorant of them during the course of their entire lives, the later apocryphal gospels, acts and epistles had a great deal of currency in the Middle Ages, when scholars had neither the will nor the academic tools to discredit them.

One of the most popular books of medieval times was *The Golden Legend,* a volume of stories about the Christian saints, by Jacobus de Voragine, a thirteenth-century archbishop of Genoa. Whereas manuscripts of some of the New Testament apocryphal texts mentioned above are extremely rare, and we have only one surviving fragment of the Gospel of Peter, there are over a thousand manuscripts of *The Golden Legend* extant, and as soon as printing became practical, versions were rushed into print.

Jacobus' 'take' on Pilate skilfully combines elements from the canonical gospels, the New Testament apocrypha and later stories. The archbishop also fills in some missing details about Pilate's early life, telling us that he was the illegitimate son of a king, with an unfortunate tendency to murder other young men who provoked his jealousy.

The Golden Legend also explains the origin of the enmity between Pilate and Herod that is mentioned by Luke. This, the archbishop tells us, stemmed from Pilate's bribing his way into the job of prefect of Judea, when Herod would rather have appointed him personally.

6. Speaking Stones

Although some medieval readers no doubt believed every word of the version of Pilate presented in Jacobus de Voragine's *Golden Legend*, in the twenty-first century we are more sceptical about such things, and more aware of how what we might call Christian mythology evolved in Europe, starting in the first few centuries after Christ. A roughly chronological review of the sources relating to Pontius Pilate, such as that attempted in the chapters above, can therefore seem like a journey from the likely and the well-known to the surreal and the fanciful.

A twenty-first century diversion from this path to the bizarre and the magical is provided by modern archaeology and historical research, both of which have a great deal to say about the world shared by Pilate and Jesus.

The most important archaeological find relating to Pontius Pilate is undoubtedly the Pilate Stone, a limestone block nearly three feet high, which was discovered by archaeologists at Caesarea in 1961.

The block had been used as part of a staircase built in the fourth century, which was attached to an older theatre built by Herod the Great, the grandfather of the Herod Antipas who reigned in Galilee when Pilate was prefect of Judea. To judge by the Latin inscription, part of which has been lost, the stone had originally been the dedication stone of a building put up at Caesarea by Pilate himself.

The inscription stretches over four lines, and all that is left of it are fragments of Latin words and a name: 'S TIBERIÉUM / NTIUS PILATUS / ECTUS IUDA E / E'. By looking at the way these words are spaced, and using their knowledge of similar inscriptions found all over the Roman world, experts have conjectured that the inscription originally read 'DIS AUGUSTIS TIBERIÉUM / PONTIUS PILATUS / PRAEFECTUS IUDAEAE / FECIT DE DICAVIT', which means 'Pontius Pilate, Prefect of Judea, has dedicated this Tiberieum to the Divine Augustus'. Scholars of the Latin language were particularly excited by this inscription because it was the first time they had seen the word 'Tiberieum', which is thought to refer to a lost temple devoted to the emperor Tiberius, dedicated and perhaps built on the orders of Pilate himself.

In theory, Roman emperors were not supposed to be worshipped as gods, or to have temples dedicated to them, until they were deified after death. In practice, however, emperors could become the object of worship during their lives, something that, as we have seen, Tiberius's successor Caligula was very keen to encourage.

From the short inscription on the Pilate Stone we can deduce a whole new story featuring Pontius Pilate as its central character.

The Prefect, who is thought to have spent most of his time in Judea at Caesarea, and only came into Jerusalem at times of stress such as the Passover festival, was familiar with the impressive Augusteum or temple to Augustus that had been built at Caesarea by Herod the Great. This temple, which was recorded by Josephus, was one of three Augusteums built by Herod to commemorate a visit the first emperor made to Judea in 20 BC. As Josephus writes in his *Jewish Antiquities*:

And when he returned home after escorting Caesar to the sea, he erected to him a very beautiful temple of white stone in the territory of Zenodorus, near the place called Paneion.

(Jewish Antiquities, 15, 363)

There are several archaeological sites in the area that may have been this Augusteum, and the place was so impressive that an image of it even featured on a coin minted under Herod the Great's son, Herod Philip. From the coin, it would seem that the temple was a fairly typical Graeco-Roman 'tetrastyle' temple with four sides and rows of columns, similar in shape to the famous Parthenon in Athens, a building such as the Greeks and the Romans left all over the Mediterranean and beyond.

Pilate, whose attempts to introduce forbidden Pagan imagery into Jerusalem have already been noted, may have worshipped at one of more of the Augusteums in Judea: the fact that the offending standards that he smuggled into the holy city of the Jews featured graven images of the emperor Tiberius may even suggest that the Prefect's personal brand of Paganism leaned towards emperor-worship.

Having perhaps personally met Tiberius, maybe when the emperor appointed him as prefect of Judea, and feeling a deep sense of obligation to him as his patron, Pilate may have been inspired by the example of the local Augusteums to build something new – a 'Tiberieum' or temple to Tiberius.

Over time, Pilate's Tiberieum may have become disused and dilapidated, and was finally used as a source for old stones to put into new buildings, such as the extension to Herod the Great's theatre.

The Pilate Stone has been so badly knocked about over the centuries that it is now hard to say whether it was well-made in the first place, but the inscription is certainly not of the first quality: it lacks the noble regularity of the best Roman inscriptions on stone, the style of which has become an icon of Roman civilisation. The capital 'I' in 'PILATUS' is far too tall, and not enough space has been allowed for the 'T', so that the horizontal part of this letter overhangs the letters on either side. If the whole Tiberieum had been made to this mediocre standard, then it may have been more of an embarrassing monument to Pilate's meanness or lack of funds than to his Pagan piety and patriotic devotion.

If nothing else, the Pilate Stone would seem to be proof, beyond the gospels and other near-contemporary records, that Pontius Pilate existed, and was a prefect of Judea who built a temple to Tiberius.

We might ask how Pilate was able to make such an obvious, lasting Pagan statement as his Tiberieum in Judea, when many of the local Jews were resistant to the worship of any gods other than Jehovah, and even objected to the inscribed shields or plaques that Pilate had had installed in his own palace in Jerusalem. The answer is that Caesarea was not the holy city of Jerusalem, and at that time it had a large number of non-Jewish citizens, and many Jews who may have regarded themselves as more Roman than Jewish. The reader may recall that when both Pilate's offending plaques and his standards were removed from Jerusalem, they were returned to Caesarea where, it is implied, their presence was quite acceptable.

Another possible memory of Pilate in stone is the 'Arrub aqueduct, which may be a rebuilt but now ruined version of the controversial aqueduct the Prefect is supposed to have funded by misusing sacred money from the Temple. The 'Arrub aqueduct carried water on a circuitous route over (and sometimes through) hills and valleys for nearly twenty-five miles.

As well as public works, Pilate was responsible for issuing coins, and examples of his coinage still survive from the years 29, 30 and 31 AD; in other words from around the time when Jesus first encountered the Roman prefect. We know, not least from the Gospel of Mark, that coins bearing images of the Roman emperor were circulating in Judea in Pilate's time: in Mark 12:16 Jesus is shown a Roman coin, and asks a question to which he already knows the answer; 'Whose image is this?'

Despite the widespread use of such coins, Pilate seems to have felt that he could not show his own image or that of the emperor on the coins he had struck at Jerusalem. These coins do, however, include Pagan imagery: the simpulum (a kind of ladle used in Pagan temples), the wreath of victory, an augur's staff or lituus, and a design made up of three ears of barley. The depictions of the simplulum and lituus in particular may not have pleased observant Jews: these images may have been intended as Roman equivalents of the Jewish use of images of menorahs, or Jewish candlesticks, in their own designs.

Although the dedication of Pilate's Tiberieaum is in Latin, the lettering on Pilate's coins is all Greek, and they are dated using a Greek numbering system. The texts all refer to the Emperor Tiberius and his wife, Julia.

The prohibition on the use of images of humans or animals on coins and military standards, at least inside the holy city of Jerusalem, evidently extended to the interior decoration of houses and palaces in that city. Where grand houses from this period have been excavated in Jerusalem, high-quality wall-paintings and mosaic floors are sometimes found, but these only show geometrical and plant-based designs.

If it is true that Pilate lived in Herod's old palace when he stayed in Jerusalem, and that the Jews would not even let him put up inscribed metal plaques in there, then Pilate's Jerusalem home-from-home would probably have lacked any of the familiar decorations of a grand Roman house elsewhere in the empire. No images of gods, goddesses, dolphins, fishermen, dancing-girls or mythical beasts such as are found at Pompeii. How at home could Pilate really have felt without such familiar imagery?

Contemplating his comparatively plain quarters, Pilate might have reflected that all the real architectural magnificence in Jerusalem was concentrated in its Temple. The Temple compound dominated the city from its hill, and glittered with gold fittings and other treasures.

Archaeological evidence from the city of Pompeii, which became a tragic time-capsule when it was buried by volcanic ash in AD 79, can be combined with information from other sites, and from surviving Roman art, architecture, literature and history to give an idea of the feel of the Roman cultural elements that surrounded Pilate. Whereas in many medieval pictures Pilate is shown wearing the colourful robes of some exotic oriental potentate, more modern paintings, and also the many screen representations of Pilate, show him either in Roman armour or in the toga, the characteristic costume of the powerful Roman male.

Since *La Vie et la Passion de Jesus Christ*, a French silent film released in 1905, Pilate's soldiers have often been shown in the familiar Roman armour and uniforms associated with the Italian legions. In fact, Pilate would have found himself commanding forces drawn largely from non-Jewish groups in the local area: Idumeans, Samarians and Syrians, who may have been all too keen to be deployed against the Jews.

Perhaps Pilate, with his literally religious reverence for the Roman emperor, had the typical condescending attitude of an imperial governor to this mixture of non-Romans, seeing them as the Latin poet Virgil saw Mark Antony's troops:

Rang'd on the line oppos'd, Antonius brings
Barbarian aids, and troops of Eastern kings;
Th' Arabians near, and Bactrians from afar,
Of tongues discordant, and a mingled war

(from Book VIII of John Dryden's translation of Virgil's *Aeneid*, 1697)

If Pilate felt any racial or national superiority in relation to the locals, this may have been complicated by his sense of his own racial identity. One of his names – Pontius – suggests that he was a member of the ancient family of the Pontii, who were Italian but not Roman in origin, having started out in Samnium in central Italy. The Samnites had fought against Rome, but had ultimately been beaten as the city on the Tiber spread her influence. As a defeated race, they were regarded with scorn by many Romans, who thought of them as country bumpkins.

Sometimes feature films that involve Pilate imply that he is backed by a vast army, giving him freedom to act as he wishes, but in fact he may have had as few as four thousand men at his disposal. And he was far from all-powerful in the region: the Roman governors of Syria were considered to be much more important, and of course it was one of these, Vitellius, who treated Pilate like a disgraced employee and sent him back to Rome because of his brutal treatment of the Samaritans. Other nearby regions were controlled by Herod Antipas and his brother Philip, representatives of a dynasty of Idumean origin that tried to embrace Judaism, Graeco-Roman culture, wealth, political power and self-interest all at the same time. Other nearby places were independent of, or not ruled directly by, Rome.

Even within Judea itself, Pilate's power was limited by the fact that he was expected to be at least aware of the concerns of the Jewish authorities; as he learned to his cost after the protests over the standards, the plaques and the aqueduct. To a man like Pilate, from the equestrian or knightly class of the Roman hierarchy, who may have earned his name Pilatus because of his skill in battle with the spear or *pilum*, the protests of the local Jews must sometimes have seemed like transparent power-plays. Let's embarrass the Prefect, he probably imagined the Jews whispering to each other behind his back. Let's report him to the governor of Syria, and then to the emperor himself.

The fact that the Jerusalem Temple hierarchy seemed to be able to stir up, and also control and weaponise, crowds of angry locals, must have been particularly alarming to Pilate, especially during festivals like Passover, when Jerusalem became crowded with pilgrims, and he personally was supposed to take up residence and maintain order. Reports of riots getting out of hand, and blood hitting the streets, could also get into letters sent back to Pilate's Roman masters, and might make him seem like something other than a safe pair of hands.

The prospect of hostile reports reaching the ears of Tiberius must have been a very worrying one for Pilate. The Emperor was a bitter, cruel, unpredictable and depraved man, not above murdering people he perceived as his enemies, even if they were relatives. His behaviour towards the Roman Jews in 19 AD was a case of using a crime committed by a handful of Jewish con-men as an excuse to send four thousand Jewish men of military age to fight the lawless bandits of the fever-ridden island of Sardinia; and to kill an even larger number who refused to serve. Those Jews not suitable to be drafted into the army were banished from the whole of Italy, unless they abjured their faith.

The story of the journey Pilate is supposed to have taken to Rome to be confronted by the rage of Tiberius after the death of Jesus, which is recounted in some of the apocryphal texts, does not take into account the fact that the emperor was seldom in Rome in those days, preferring to indulge his sexual perversions on Capri while the empire was left in the hands of an ambitious soldier of the equestrian class, Lucius Aelius Sejanus. Given the influence Sejanus exercised from 26 AD, the year when Tiberius left Rome and Pilate may have been appointed as prefect of Judea, it is quite possible that Pilate's appointment had a great deal to do with

Sejanus. The Prefect would therefore have wanted to keep in the good books of both of these powerful, dangerous men.

When he heard of the fall from power and subsequent execution of Sejanus in 31 AD, Pilate might have been concerned that his fortunes might also change; but he remained Prefect of Judea until 36 AD.

It may be that circumstances surrounding the rise and fall of Sejanus provide the historical answer to one of the greatest puzzles concerning Pontius Pilate. As we have seen, it is hard to reconcile the Pilate of the Gospel of John, who tries so hard to save Jesus from the cross, with the Pilate of Josephus and Philo of Alexandria, a man who is accused of trying to destroy the Jewish religion, and at least seems to have deliberately tried to provoke the Jews with his offending standards, and plaques, and his appropriation of Temple money.

It is possible that Pilate was a harsher prefect, especially to the local observant Jews, when Sejanus was at the height of his power; and a more moderate and sensitive prefect after Sejanus' fall, when, near-contemporary historians tell us, the newly re-emergent Emperor Tiberius saw through the baseless accusations Sejanus had brought against the Jews, rolled back his anti-Jewish policies, and declared that the Jews should no longer be persecuted.

This theory, that Pilate changed his attitude to the Jewish population when Tiberius regained control of his empire from the Jew-hating Sejanus, has implications for our dating of Jesus' Passion, and implies that John's version of Pilate should be taken at face value, and not as an attempt to whitewash Pilate in order to throw more blame onto the Jews.

If John's Pilate is therefore a pragmatist, carefully swaying with each new political wind, he still may not deserve the sympathy shown to him in some later, often strongly anti-Semitic, accounts. Some of the explanation for this bizarre championing of Pilate may be to do with the determination of John's generation of Christians to look west to Europe and embrace Gentile, and specifically Roman and Greek, converts. The strategy paid off, because it enabled Christianity to survive the devastation visited on Pilate's old bailiwick by the Romans around 70 AD; and eventually the Roman Empire became the means by which the religion of Jesus conquered Europe.

But today many commentators regret that by favouring European ways the spreading tree of Christianity broke off from its Jewish roots and began to grow the strange, poisonous fruit of anti-Semitism.

7. What is Truth?

The possibility that Pilate, as an imperial prefect, was able to sense changes in official Roman attitudes towards the Jews, from his base in Judea, over two thousand miles away from Rome, when the only means of communication were letters brought by ships and post-horses, may seem unlikely; but this ability to read the runes at long distance, and to control the flow of news in the other direction, would have been an essential part of the skill-set of any imperial official who wanted to survive and stay in office, even under Tiberius, who changed his far-flung prefects only infrequently.

The need for such a skill, which almost seems like a species of long-range telepathy, was one of the characteristics of Roman life at this time, which also exhibited other symptoms that tend to afflict empires. In her book on Pilate, Ann Wroe enthusiastically compares features of Pilate's world to aspects of the far more recent British Empire: this sort of comparison should only be attempted with caution, but if it is done at all it should also encompass more recent attempts at another kind of empire, such as NATO, and the 'soft power' and world policing of the modern United States.

Visitors to U.S. military bases in Europe and elsewhere are often astonished to see how American they are, with U.S.-style shops, diners, bars and cinemas which seem to turn a corner of Berkshire, for instance, into a clone of a suburb of somewhere like Milwaukee. In the context of this book, one is reminded of Caesarea in Pilate's time, with its Roman, Pagan features and its air of being a little Rome.

The difference is that, whereas the locals' access to U.S. bases is restricted, Caesarea in its heyday sucked in citizens from many different places, including locals of different ethnicities and beliefs. Seeing Jews, Romans, Greeks, Samarians, Idumeans and others mixing together in the city's public spaces, an optimistic observer might have imagined that this was an example of a successfully diverse culture, free from prejudice or tribalism. But not everybody thought that Caesarea was the answer to Judea's problems. Writing much later, Rabbi Isaac Napaha of Caesarea, whose comments are recorded in the Talmud, implied that Caesarea and Jerusalem were rivals and opposites, and that anything that was good for Caesarea was bad for Jerusalem, and vice versa.

Perhaps the true nature of Caesarea was revealed during the Roman war against the Jews of 66-70 AD. Vespasian, who later became emperor, turned the city into his garrison and base of operations, stationing something like ten thousand soldiers there. This Jewish War was a response to a Jewish revolt, and such moments, when the iron fist inside the velvet glove is revealed, are also characteristic of empire. While some idealistic imperialists imagine that they are bringing peace, prosperity, progress, freedom, security and even a superior culture and belief system to the areas they overrun, the constant presence of the tax-collector and the garrison soldier are reminders that the darker aspects of the imperial project are always lurking just below the surface.

Implied in the attitudes of many imperialists throughout history, even the attitudes of those who are anxious about the welfare of their imperial subjects, is a belief in their own innate superiority and right to rule foreign nations. Did Pontius Pilate believe that the Romans, who had brutally suppressed his own Samnite people, were superior? Was his ill-conceived aqueduct scheme a ham-fisted attempt to show what wonderful things the Romans could do for Jerusalem? Did he really think that the Jews of Jerusalem would be better off if they abandoned Jehovah, or made him a member of a wider pantheon of Pagan gods? Did he think that introducing graven images would enrich the cultural life of these people?

Even if we think of Pilate as well-meaning, we must admit that he struggled to understand the strange, un-European, monotheistic culture that surrounded him when he was in Jerusalem. It is quite possible that he would have felt more at home in the later Christian culture of medieval Europe. Here, many Pagan elements had been added to a religion which had started out as a minority Jewish sect. A time-travelling Pilate, visiting medieval churches in modern Europe, might mistake them for Pagan temples, or places of worship devoted to some syncretic hybrid of Judaism and the worship of the ancient Roman gods. Is that fresco of a bearded man descending from heaven supposed to represent Jehovah or Jupiter? Why are there so many Latin inscriptions all over the place? Why do the priests wear the garb of Byzantine courtiers? Who are these other gods and goddesses; the lady with the blue veil, and the old man holding the oversized set of keys? What animals do they sacrifice on that altar? And are those *military standards* hanging up in that chapel? Those statues of kings and emperors – are people worshipping them?

It may be that Pilate's famous question about truth will never be satisfactorily answered when it is applied to Pilate himself. What is the truth about Pilate, and what can we say for sure about him? He remains a puzzle and a paradox partly because the authors of the sources we rely on for his biography had their own agendas and could not but be partial in their treatment. Writing in the character of a deeply concerned Herod Antipas to the Emperor Caligula, Philo of Alexandria holds Pilate up as an example of how Caligula's predecessors would not have trampled all over Jewish sensitivities; and Josephus' treatment of Pilate also seems to be part of an object-lesson in how Rome should govern Judea.

In the gospels, particularly John, with its very detailed treatment of Pilate, we may be seeing the beginnings of Christianity's attempt to woo potential European believers by showing the one named European directly involved in the Passion narrative in a sympathetic light. It is to be hoped that in our post-colonial times, when the political, industrial and cultural hegemony of the west is severely challenged, feelings about the innate superiority of pale males will not colour our opinion of the man who crucified Jesus.

8. Appendix: Josephus on Pilate: From the Jewish Antiquities, Chapters 3 & 4, trans. Whiston

But now Pilate, the procurator of Judea, removed the army from Caesarea to Jerusalem, to take their winter quarters there, in order to abolish the Jewish laws. So he introduced Caesar's effigies, which were upon the ensigns, and brought them into the city; whereas our law forbids us the very making of images; on which account the former procurators were wont to make their entry into the city with such ensigns as had not those ornaments. Pilate was the first who brought those images to Jerusalem, and set them up there; which was done without the knowledge of the people, because it was done in the night time; but as soon as they knew it, they came in multitudes to Caesarea, and interceded with Pilate many days that he would remove the images; and when he would not grant their requests, because it would tend to the injury of Caesar, while yet they persevered in their request, on the sixth day he ordered his soldiers to have their weapons privately, while he came and sat upon his judgement-seat, which seat was so prepared in the open place of the city, that it concealed the army that lay ready to oppress them; and when the Jews petitioned him again, he gave a signal to the soldiers to encompass them routed, and threatened that their punishment should be no less than immediate death, unless they would leave off disturbing him, and go their ways home. But they threw themselves upon the ground, and laid their necks bare, and said they would take their death very willingly, rather than the wisdom of their laws should be transgressed; upon which Pilate was deeply affected with their firm resolution to keep their laws inviolable, and presently commanded the images to be carried back from Jerusalem to Caesarea.

But Pilate undertook to bring a current of water to Jerusalem, and did it with the sacred money, and derived the origin of the stream from the distance of two hundred furlongs. However, the Jews were not pleased with what had been done about this water; and many ten thousands of the people got together, and made a clamour against him, and insisted that he should leave off that design. Some of them also used reproaches, and abused the man, as crowds of such people usually do. So he habited a great number of his soldiers in their habit, who carried daggers under their garments, and sent them to a place where they might surround them. So he bid the Jews himself go away; but they boldly casting reproaches upon him, he gave the soldiers that signal which had been beforehand agreed on; who laid upon them much greater blows than Pilate had commanded them, and equally punished those that were tumultuous, and those that were not; nor did they spare them in the least: and since the people were unarmed, and were caught by men prepared for what they were about, there were a great number of them slain by this means, and others of them ran away wounded. And thus an end was put to this sedition . . .

But the nation of the Samaritans did not escape without tumults. The man who excited them to it was one who thought lying a thing of little consequence, and who contrived every thing so that the multitude might be pleased; so he bid them to get together upon Mount Gerizzim, which is by them looked upon as the most holy of all mountains, and assured them, that when they were come thither, he would show them those sacred vessels which were laid under that place, because Moses put them there So they came thither armed, and thought the discourse of the man probable; and as they abode at a certain village, which was called Tirathaba, they got the rest together to them, and desired to go up the mountain in a great multitude together; but Pilate prevented their going up, by seizing upon file roads with a great band of horsemen and foot-men, who fell upon those that were gotten together in the village; and when it came to an action, some of them they slew, and others of them they put to flight, and took a great many alive, the principal of which, and also the most potent of those that fled away, Pilate ordered to be slain.

But when this tumult was appeased, the Samaritan senate sent an embassy to Vitellius, a man that had been consul, and who was now president of Syria, and accused Pilate of the murder of those that were killed; for that they did not go to Tirathaba in order to revolt from the Romans, but to escape the violence of Pilate. So Vitellius sent Marcellus, a friend of his, to take care of the affairs of Judea, and ordered Pilate to go to Rome, to answer before the emperor to the accusations of the Jews. So Pilate, when he had tarried ten years in Judea, made haste to Rome, and this in obedience to the orders of Vitellius, which he durst not contradict; but before he could get to Rome Tiberius was dead.

Select Bibliography

Dowson, Ernest Christopher: *A Comedy of Masks*, Forgotten Books, 2017

Evans, Craig A.: *Jesus and His World*, SPCK, 2012

Grant, Robert M.: *A Historical Introduction to the New Testament*, Collins, 1963

Green, Joel B.: *The Gospel of Luke*, Eerdmans, 1997

Holum, Kenneth G. et al: *King Herod's Dream: Caesarea on the Sea*, Norton, 1987

James, M.R. (trans.): *The Apocryphal New Testament*, Oxford, 1953

Jones, A.H.M.: *The Herods of Judaea*, Oxford, 1938

Josephus: *Jewish Antiquities*, Wordsworth, 2006

Josephus: *The Jewish War*, Penguin, 1959

Lindars, Barnabas: *John*, JSOT, 1990

Marshall, Alfred (ed.): *The Interlinear Greek-English New Testament*, Samuel Bagster, 1959

Pfeiffer, Robert H: *History of New Testament Times*, Adam and Charles Black, 1949

Philo Judaeus (trans. Charles Yonge): *Works*, Bohn, 1854-5

Plutarch: *The Fall of the Roman Republic*, Penguin, 1972

Pummer, Reinhard: *The Samaritans: A Profile*, Eerdmans, 2016

Rieu, E.V. (trans.): *The Four Gospels*, Penguin, 1952

Ritmeyer, Leen and Kathleen: *Jerusalem in the Year 30 AD*, Carta, 2015

Roberts, Alexander and Donaldson, James (eds.): *The Anti-Nicene Fathers* Vol VIII, Eerdmans, 1951

Smallwood, E. Mary: *The Jews Under Roman Rule*, Brill, 2001

Suetonius: *The Twelve Caesars*, Penguin, 2003

Tacitus: *Annals*, Oxford, 2008

Wroe, Ann: *Pilate: The Biography of an Invented Man*, Jonathan Cape, 1999

What Do We Know About
Caiaphas?

1. The Bone-Box

In November 1990, builders working at the Peace Park to the south of Jerusalem came upon an ancient underground tomb when their bulldozer sank into its roof. In plan, the tomb was found to resemble a human right hand spread out palm down, but with only three fingers pointing north-west, while an elongated thumb pointed south-west. In one of these digits, investigators found the bones of a man called Caiaphas.

The tomb, which had probably been cut out of the living rock some two thousand years ago, was modest in size: the distance from the tip of the 'thumb' to the tip of the little finger was less than twenty feet. The digits, each of which stretched about six feet from the 'palm', were narrow niches, known as *kokhim* or *loculi*, of the type in which, at one time, Jewish corpses would have been laid to rest and left undisturbed, except by tomb-robbers, for all eternity.

But as western habits began to have more influence over the lives of Jews living in Judea in the first century CE, it became the custom to re-visit bodies a year after they had been entombed, gather up the bones (which would have been pretty much all that was left by that time) and place these in ossuaries or bone-boxes. Unlike conventional coffins in the west, it seems that there was no rule that stated that there had to be just one set of bones per box. If there was room, the bones of several individuals would be placed in the box. As new sets of bones were added, the names of the relevant individuals would be scratched into the soft stone of the outside of the box. All of the intact ossuaries in the Peace Park tomb contained the bones of more than one person: one ossuary even contained the bones of eleven people.

The Jews had adapted the use of ossuaries from the Roman practice of cremating bodies, picking the bones out of the ashes and placing those in bone-boxes. Since cremation was forbidden by Jewish law, the Jews relied on decomposition to strip the bones.

In 2000, researchers found the body of a Jew from the time of Jesus sealed in a tomb in the ancient cemetery of Akeldama in Jerusalem, a place associated in the New Testament with Judas Iscariot, who betrayed Jesus. The occupant of the so-called Tomb of the Shroud was lying full-length, and his bones had not been placed in an ossuary. By chance, conditions had preserved some of the hair and skin of this man, and analysis revealed that he had been suffering from tuberculosis, and had died from the complications of leprosy (now known as Hansen's disease). This find suggests that, in cases where the dead person was known to have had an infectious disease, the ossuary procedure would be skipped.

It is likely that if the ossuary habit had spread to ancient Britain, the bone-boxes themselves would have been made of wood, which would have been cheaper, more plentiful, quicker and easier to work, and also lighter in use than stone. Wood was not so plentiful in ancient Judea as it was in ancient Britain with its vast, dark primeval forests. As Solomon discovered when he wanted to use cedar for his Temple, the best wood had to be imported into the Holy Land (see 1 Kings 5-6).

The fact that the Jews of the first century made their ossuaries out of stone is, of course, good news for archaeologists. Israel is not Egypt, where the intensely dry conditions can preserve wooden items by a process of dessication (which can, however, render them extremely vulnerable and in need of careful restoration). In Judea, wood was more likely to rot away, but the stone of the ancient ossuaries is not only not subject to such decay: it also builds up a surface patina over the centuries that researchers can use to determine the age of the bone-box in question. This is useful, since the well-know radiocarbon or carbon 14 dating method only works on organic matter – not on stone. Hundreds of these ancient Jewish ossuaries have been recovered in the Holy Land, not all of them by legitimate means. There are now so many that a large number have to be warehoused, and there is no room to display them all in museums. Any bones found in them, or out of ossuaries in the tombs, are given a respectful Jewish re-burial.

As well as good news for archaeologists, the use of stone for ossuaries in ancient Judea was a boon for the Jewish stone-masons of the time. These craftsmen, particularly the ones who specialised in making portable stone objects, would probably have been kept very busy by the demands of the Jewish market in any case: the Jews preferred drinking vessels, jars and bowls for washing and the like to be made of stone, because this material was believed to be more resistant to ritual contamination than pottery. The Jews of the time often felt obliged to throw pottery items away when they believed them to have become ritually contaminated.

The tomb found in 1990 in the Jerusalem Peace Park contained twelve ossuaries, but only four were found to be intact by archaeologists sent by the Israel Antiquities Authority. At some point, the tomb had been trashed by grave-robbers, but one of the four intact ossuaries, dubbed ossuary six, was soon to become the most famous bone-box in the world. This was a box, the largest found in the tomb, fashioned from soft limestone, that measured about fourteen and a half by twenty-nine and a half inches. It contained some of the bones of six people: four children, an adult woman and a man in his sixties. Although the box was carved with beautiful, intricate designs, parts of which were originally painted orange, the experts were probably more interested in the two names that had been crudely scratched on two of the plain, undecorated surfaces of the outside: these read 'Yehoseph bar Qyp' and 'Yehoseph bar Qp' respectively.

Experts have speculated that both of these names may refer to the same person – the man known to readers of the New Testament as Caiaphas, and to readers of the first-century Jewish historian Josephus as *Joseph* Caiaphas, whose name would have been pronounced 'Qapha' in Aramaic (the version 'Caiaphas' is the Aramaic name rendered into Greek, the language in which the New Testament has come down to us).

Although he had been high priest of the Temple at Jerusalem, and was therefore an important historical character in his own right, Caiaphas is remembered today as one of the men whose actions brought about the crucifixion of Jesus Christ.

The dating of a coin and some pottery found in the Peace Garden tomb, the tomb's location in a high-status necropolis, and the rich decoration on the ossuary itself also point to the possibility that 'Qp' and 'Qyp' here may both refer to the Caiaphas of the New Testament.

Aramaic, the language of the crude inscriptions, is, however, written without vowels, so that 'Qp' and 'Qyp' may denote a name other than 'Caiaphas': Qopha is another possibility. But the inscription on an ossuary from another tomb, recovered in 2011, suggests that the way 'Caiaphas' was written on ossuary six from the tomb discovered in 1990 was indeed a way 'Caiaphas' could be written.

The 2011 ossuary was not found *in situ* but plundered in modern times from another tomb. Its inscription reads, in

79

part, 'Miriam, daughter of Yeshua, son of Caiaphas, priest': in other words, the 2011 ossuary belonged to a granddaughter of a man with the unusual nick-name of Caiaphas, who was a priest. The ossuary of another Miriam, a niece of Caiaphas, has also been found.

The style of the inscription, the nature of the decoration on the so-called Miriam ossuary, and the likely dates of two oil-lamps apparently found with the box, together with careful examination of its surface, all suggest that it might indeed have contained the bones of a grand-daughter of Caiaphas, the high priest of the first century CE who features in Josephus, the New Testament gospels and the Book of Acts.

Although the inscription on the Miriam ossuary seems to back up the idea that 'Qp' and 'Qyp' could be ways of writing 'Caiaphas', there are other objections to the theory that the so-called Caiaphas ossuary had anything to do with the Caiaphas of the New Testament. Wasn't the tomb it was found in rather small and crude to be associated with an important man like a high priest? Wasn't a coin found inside the skull of yet another Miriam, who was buried in the same tomb? Doesn't this relate to a Pagan custom, the pennies left on the eyes of the dead so that they could pay Charon, the ferryman of Hades? Would a relative of a Jewish high priest embrace such a Pagan custom? And if the 'Qp' or 'Qyp' of the ossuary was once a high priest, why wasn't this fact mentioned on the ossuary's inscription? After all, the Miriam of the ossuary recovered in 2011 was identified in her inscription as both the daughter and granddaughter of priests.

The comparative modesty of the Peace Garden tomb can be explained by the fact that, although he was high priest of the Temple for a time, Caiaphas's own family, among whom he would have wished to be buried, was not of the very highest status, and may not have been particularly large. The discovery of the coin, which dates from the forties CE, may merely indicate that although he had been a distinguished religious figure in the Jewish tradition, not everybody in his family was a stickler about avoiding Pagan practices. The lack of a job-title in the 'Qyp' inscription can also be explained with reference to the fact that, although the Miriam ossuary recovered in 2011 gave the job titles of Miriam's father and grandfather, most of the inscriptions on ossuaries of this type do not include that kind of information. And we know that, some time before he died, Caiaphas had lost his position as high priest.

Decades of investigative surveys and excavations, building, re-building, development and demolition in the Holy Land have allowed archaeologists to bring to light a number of objects and structures that relate to events, locations and characters familiar to readers of the New Testament and Josephus.

If we believe that the Miriam ossuary did indeed contain the bones of the granddaughter of the New Testament Caiaphas, then the rest of the inscription on that box informs us that both Caiaphas the priest and his son Yeshua had belonged to 'Ma'aziah', one of the priestly 'courses' or work-groups of the Temple; and that they came from 'Beth'Imri', which may be either a place-name or the name of a family.

Similar information can be gleaned from such finds as the so-called Pilate Stone, discovered at the ancient port city of Caesarea Maritima on the Mediterranean coast in 1961. As well as bearing an inscription including the name PONTIUS PILATUS, the stone also tells us that Pilate built a 'TIBERIEUM', some sort of temple dedicated to the Roman emperor Tiberius.

While some very informative artefacts, such as the ossuaries mentioned above, have been discovered in fairly recent times, the remains of buildings that may have a New Testament connection have in some cases been known about for rather longer. Among these would be two houses in Nazareth, thought to have been the respective childhood homes of Jesus and his mother; and a house at Capernaum, on the northern shore of the Sea of Galilee, thought to have belonged to St Peter. It seems that this house had been converted into a simple church in the first century CE; and more Christian building followed in the fourth and fifth centuries. At some point, however, these buildings fell into disuse and the significance of the site was forgotten, until archaeologists uncovered it in the 1960s.

Among more recent discoveries are the so-called 'Jesus boat', a craft perhaps similar to those used by St Peter and his comrades, who were of course fishermen. Dating from their period, this remarkable vessel made of cedar wood, preserved in the mud under the Sea of Galilee for over two thousand years, was discovered when a drought lowered the level of the Sea in 1986.

More controversial finds include the so-called First Talpiot tomb, uncovered by builders, like the Caiaphas Tomb, but in 1980. Some still believe this to have been the tomb of Jesus Christ and members of his family, including even his wife and children, which, if proved, would contradict many ideas about the Galilean that have been cherished by Christians for centuries. In the Middle Ages in particular, the idea of the single, virginal state of Jesus, and of his mother, was fiercely defended. Even if examination of the contents of the Talpiot tomb did not suggest that the Yeshua or Jesus buried there was married and had fathered children, the idea that the bones of Christ may have lain there still contradicts Christian beliefs. Forty days after his crucifixion and resurrection, Jesus is supposed to have ascended bodily into heaven (see Acts 1:9-11).

Much scholarly discussion of the significance of the First Talpiot tomb centres around a cross marked near the name 'Yeshua' or Jesus found on one of the ossuaries, and the symbol carved above the entrance to the tomb. Experts who are convinced that the first Talpiot tomb contains Jesus of Nazareth and his family believe that the cross marked on the ossuary is a Christian symbol, but others maintain that it is a mark put there so that the lid of the ossuary could be put on the right way round. While some say that the symbol above the tomb entrance – a circle with an inverted 'V' above it, is distinctively Christian, others point out that the symbol was widely used by Jews and Gentiles alike well before Jesus came on the scene.

If Jesus and his family were indeed buried in the first Talpiot tomb, one would expect his brother James to have been buried there as well, but the ossuary said to be James's, the existence of which was first announced in 2002, was probably discovered elsewhere. The inscription on this rather battered bone-box reads 'James, son of Joseph, brother of Jesus'. Like many of the Jewish ossuaries that have been recovered, that may have contained the bones of well-know New Testament characters, the so-called 'James ossuary' has given rise to controversy. Weighing up the arguments, Craig A. Evans, in his 2015 book *Jesus and the Remains of His Day* concludes that initial analysis of the inscription on this ossuary was misleading because somebody in modern times had gone to the trouble of cleaning the inscription, thus removing much of the all-important patina. According to Evans, re-examination of the inscription has revealed remaining traces of ancient patina, which at least suggests that the inscription was not added in modern times.

2. God's House

James the brother of Jesus, known as James the Just, whose ossuary may have been discovered by twenty-first century tomb robbers, was noted for his extreme piety. That this piety had distinctively Jewish characteristics is recorded by Eusebius of Caesarea, the fourth-century Christian historian. Eusebius, quoting the earlier chronicler Hegesippus, tells us that James refused to wear wool, and wore fine linen at all times, so that he would always be allowed to enter the Jerusalem Temple. There he spent so many hours on his knees, praying for forgiveness for the people, that his knees became horny like a camel's.

As if to show how the exalted position of high priest of the Temple was sometimes handed around among the members of a particular dynasty, James the brother of Jesus was executed on the orders of a high priest called Ananus ben Ananus, who was the earlier high priest Caiaphas's brother-in-law. The Temple played a part in James's death, as it had in his life. According to Eusebius, again quoting from Hegesippus, Jesus' brother was thrown from the top of the Temple, but did not die: it then became necessary to stone him; but still he remained alive. At last a fuller took a club – one of the tools of his trade – and finished James off with a blow to the head.

The fact that James did not die straight away, and that he fell outside the walls of the Temple complex, suggests that he was thrown from some part of the outer walls – perhaps one of the celebrated gates. This was important because nobody was supposed to be killed in those sacred precincts, and if anyone died inside, the body had to be taken out straight away to avoid ritual contamination.

The Jews' fear of contamination from dead bodies provoked a ghoulish attack on the Jerusalem Temple by the rival Samaritan religious and ethnic group during the time of the first Roman governor of Judea, Coponius. During the Passover celebrations in 9 CE a group of Samaritans gained entrance to the Temple and rendered parts of it ritually unclean by scattering human bones about the place.

Although it never seems to have made it into the 'official' list, the Jerusalem Temple James would have known, the Temple over which Caiaphas had once held so much power, was truly one of the wonders of the ancient world. Like all but one of the official seven – the Great Pyramid at Giza in Egypt, the Temple is now almost entirely lost, destroyed by the Romans in 70 CE, after their war against the Jews.

Caiaphas's Temple was known as Herod's Temple. It was not the first Jewish temple on this site to be destroyed – the first, built by King Solomon, had been taken down by the Babylonians in the fifth or sixth century BCE.

Construction of the Second Temple may have commenced shortly after the destruction of the First, when the area was controlled by the Persians. It became known as Herod's Temple after it had been re-built and greatly expanded under Herod the Great, beginning around 20 BCE. As a building, it reflected the paradoxical nature of the rule of this particular Herod and his descendants, at least in the eyes of pious Jews. The Herodians built many splendid buildings, and even cities, and turned the House of God into something truly breath-taking; but they were puppet-rulers under the control of the Pagan Romans, and both their ancestry and family culture were inconsistent with Jewish ideas of religious purity and perfection.

By the time Caiaphas became high priest of the Temple at Jerusalem, Herod the Great had been dead for perhaps twenty years, and Judea, where Jerusalem is located, was ruled by a Roman prefect. Building was still going on in parts of the Temple complex, and by this time parts of it already needed maintenance.

According to Josephus, writing in his *Jewish War*, when visitors first saw the Temple they thought they were looking at the top of a snowy mountain – the highest part of the complex shone with white marble and glittered with gold. Josephus also manages to convey his wonderment at what may have been one of the last things visitors might have noticed – the vast platform that formed the base of the entire complex. This was nearly fifteen hundred feet long and nearly a thousand feet wide, its length at its longest point being equal to the length of about twenty tennis-courts. This vast flat top to Mount Moriah, the mountain in Jerusalem on which the Temple complex had been built, was almost entirely artificial – it had been created by building up the mountain to such a great height that the Englishman Charles Wilson, who surveyed the city in 1846, wrote in his *Recovery of Jerusalem* that:

It is almost impossible to realise the effect which would be produced by a building longer and higher than York Cathedral, standing on a solid mass of masonry almost equal in height to the tallest of our church spires.

Here Wilson was not even referring to the inner Temple itself, the highest part of the complex, but only to the largest of its gates – the so-called Royal Porch, thought to have been built on the original site of Solomon's palace. Some think that it was to the top of this gate that Satan brought Jesus to tempt him, saying that if indeed he was the Son of God, then he could throw himself down and not be hurt, because angels would catch him. Other gates included the 'Beautiful Gate' which, as we shall see, is mentioned in the New Testament Book of Acts; and the Gate of Coponius, named after the first Roman governor of Judea.

The Royal Porch was just one of a number of entrances to the outer court of the Temple complex – the so-called Court of the Gentiles. Anyone could come here, as long as they behaved in a respectful manner, but they needed to heed the warnings written on prominent stone plaques about entering into the inner courts of the complex if they were ritually impure, or non-Jews. Both complete and partial versions of these plaques still exist: there is one of each. Their message is written in large Greek letters, deeply cut into the stone and originally picked out in red, and they warn that anyone who is not Jewish will be killed if they are foolish enough to proceed beyond them.

Even Jews who were thought to have brought Gentiles into the forbidden courts of the Temple could be subject to violence. Acts 21: 27-36 tells us how some Jews from Asia spotted St Paul in the Temple and accused him of bringing a Greek into a part of the Temple that was forbidden to such a man. The author of Acts explains that the Jews had seen Paul in the city with a man from Ephesus called Trophimus, and assumed that the saint had taken him into parts of the Temple that were reserved for Jews. The Jews took hold of Paul, dragged him out of the Temple, and attempted to kill him, but the Roman military commander was informed and stepped in to arrest him. This all happened after the crucifixion, resurrection and ascension of Jesus, and after Caiaphas had been removed from office, during the time as high priest of his brother-in-law, the aforementioned Ananus ben Ananus, called 'Ananais' in many English bibles.

According to Alfred Edersheim's classic study of Herod's Temple, it was in the Court of the Gentiles that Mary and Joseph found the twelve year-old Jesus listening to and asking questions of the teachers there. The Gospel of

Luke tells us that like many thousands of Jews at the time, it was the custom of Mary and Joseph to spend every Passover at Jerusalem. After the festival, the carpenter and his wife were returning home when they realised that their son was not with them. They returned to the Holy City and, after a three-day search, found him in the 'temple courts' (Lk 2:46).

Earlier, when Jesus was just forty-one days old or a little older, Mary and Joseph would have come to Jerusalem to 'redeem' their first-born son by offering a pair of sacrificial doves or pigeons. This is also recounted in Luke (2: 22-4) and had to do with God's words to Moses in the Old Testament Book of Exodus, where he claimed every first-born son for himself (Exodus 13: 2).

It was also in the Court of the Gentiles that Jesus showed his anger by overturning the tables of the money-changers and, making a whip out of chords, drove the merchants and the sellers of sacrificial animals from the Temple precincts. This incident is attested by all four gospels, and since it happened in such a public place during the crowded Passover period, the Temple authorities, and even High Priest Caiaphas himself, were bound to have heard about it.

All around the edge of the Court of the Gentiles was a deep, shady colonnade or series of porches with seats and benches inside, that must have seemed particularly inviting when it was raining, or in the heat of a summer noon at this latitude. One of these was Solomon's porch or colonnade, said to have been the one remaining part of that ancient king's Temple. Here Jesus was questioned by some Jews who were present at the time of the winter festival of Hanukkah. According to John 10: 22-39 they challenged him to reveal whether or not he was the Messiah: his answer made them want to capture him and stone him for blasphemy, but he slipped away.

The first of the inner courts that were inaccessible to Gentiles was the so-called Court of the Women. This was not reserved for women alone – it was merely the innermost court into which women were admitted. Here there were thirteen conical receptacles, called 'trumpets' because of their shape, which received money contributed to the Temple for various purposes. Trumpet number three, for instance, was for money to buy turtle-doves to be sacrificed in the Temple, while trumpets five and six received offerings for the wood for the sacrifices, and for incense, respectively.

Further in was the Court of the Israelites, for Jewish men, and even further in was the area where only priests could set foot.

The Temple priests enjoyed different status-levels based partly on their physical characteristics. Priests who were deformed or permanently maimed in some way were not permitted to serve at the giant altar that stood before the entrance to the inner sanctum or sanctuary of the Temple, and they could certainly not aspire to become a high priest. The deformities and medical conditions that debarred priests from serving in this way included blindness, pterygium (a kind of growth on the outer eye), cataracts, an excessively flat nose, hands or feet of unequal length, a hunched back, a crushed testicle, and dermatitis. One of the high priests, John Hyrcanus II, lost both of his ears because his nephew, Antigonus Mattathias, wanted to prevent him from serving as a priest. In one version of this story, Antigonus personally bit off his uncle's ears. Priests who were unlucky enough to be bow-legged, or had black skin, were albinos or bald-headed, or had any of the challenges mentioned above, or any of the ninety blemishes mentioned by the twelfth-century Spanish rabbi Maimonides, were likely to find themselves performing low-level tasks such as checking through firewood and discarding any infected with woodworm.

If nothing else, the long catalogue of health problems that excluded men from the higher ranks of the Temple priesthood suggests that Caiaphas must have been free of all these afflictions or, if he were not, was able to hide one or more of them very effectively. Certain temporary health factors could, however, exclude the high priest from some of his duties for a time. If he had had sex, or even a wet-dream, he might have to go through a period of purification before he could participate in certain rites. Some types of injuries would need to heal before he could legitimately resume the full roster of his sacred duties, and he would need to recover from ailments such as temporary skin-rashes.

As well as health and physical appearance, genetics played a part in the selection of priests, and their progress up the Temple hierarchy. The priests were part of a distinct caste, supposedly sharing a common ancestry, and carefully-preserved written genealogies were anxiously consulted before a member of the priestly caste was promoted, or got married.

The altar of unhewn stones that stood before the entrance to the most sacred building, the altar that could not be tended by physically imperfect priests, was twice the height of a tall man, and the top of it could only be reached by a system of ramps leading to a platform or 'circuit'. On the flat top of the altar, three fires burned – one of wood, one of incense and the third for sacrificed animals. The sides of the altar were regularly sprinkled with blood from the sacrifices, which were carefully checked before they were slaughtered, to ensure that they were 'unspotted' and physically perfect. The four 'horns' of the altar were used to pour liquid offerings. The 'firstlings', such as the first lambs born in the lambing season, had a special religious significance, as did the first lambs born to ewes who had never produced lambs before. Some of these ideas were adopted by the early Christians, who identified Jesus as the unspotted first-born lamb whose sacrifice was most pleasing to God, and atoned for the sins of the world. This connection is made explicit in Martin Scorsese's 1988 film based on *The Last Temptation of Christ*, a novel by the Greek writer

Nikos Kazantzakis. In the film, scenes of the sacrifice of the Passover lambs in the Temple serve to contextualise Jesus' actions at the Last Supper.

Behind the Temple altar were the most sacred spaces in the whole complex: the Holy Place and the Holy of Holies. Above the gold-plated outer doors was a giant grape-vine in solid gold, so large that the clusters of grapes were as big as a man. At one time, a Roman-style eagle adorned this entrance, but shortly after the death of Herod the Great this was removed by Jewish agitators who resented the rule of the Romans. These men climbed down from the roof of the inner Temple on ropes and removed the eagle with axes. As well as being a symbol of Roman rule, the eagle, as a depiction of an animal that was real and not mythical, also offended Jewish law, which also forbade depictions of people and gods. Mythical creatures could be depicted in the Temple – hence the two golden cherubim who stood facing each other on the Ark of the Covenant in Solomon's Temple. Even if the Roman eagle over the entrance to the central building was never restored, according to Edersheim there was still an eagle on the aforementioned Gate of Coponius, named after the first Roman governor of Judea.

In the 1965 biblical epic film *The Greatest Story Ever Told*, there is evidence, particularly towards the beginning of the film, that the screen-writers had read their Josephus, but here the eagle that is cut down by Jewish rebels stands over the entrance to Pilate's house in Jerusalem. This is an occasion that is not recorded in Josephus, but may be a conflation of a number of events related to Pilate's time as prefect of Judea.

Through the door that led under the gold grape-vine, which did not offend Jewish laws against 'graven images', were a giant gold candlestick, a table for the shewbread (an offering of bread that was replaced every week) and an altar for incense. Beyond this room was the Holy of Holies, separated from the first section of the room by a wooden partition and a curtain. This curtain was the 'veil of the Temple' that, according to the gospel of Matthew, was split in two at the moment of Jesus' death on the cross, an event which also coincided with both an earthquake that split open rocks, and the resurrections of many holy people, who rose from their tombs and walked into Jerusalem.

If the miraculous splitting or rending of the curtain caused it to gape open, this must have caused considerable consternation among any priests who witnessed this event, or discovered the damaged curtain next morning. Not only was the high priest the only one allowed to enter the Holy of Holies, and that only once a year – he was also the only one allowed to *look* inside. One of his duties was to examine the sacred space without entering it, from a hatch in the ceiling, to check if any maintenance was needed – but this was done only once every seven years, and the tenure of some high priests of Herod's Temple was so short that they never had an opportunity to do it. If repairs were needed, it was important that the workmen did not get a good look at the whole chamber, so they were lowered down in boxes that allowed them to see only the parts of the room that they had to work on.

The one occasion in the Jewish religious year when the high priest was permitted to pass through the curtain into the Holy of Holies was during the Yom Kippur festival, when he sprinkled sacrificial blood on the stone that stood inside in the place of the Ark of the Covenant. The Ark itself had been taken and probably destroyed by the Babylonian king Nebuchadnezzar in the sixth century BCE, although there are other theories about its ultimate fate, its survival and current location. Its absence was one of the factors that made Herod's Temple inferior to the ancient Temple of Solomon, despite its astonishing size and magnificence.

Before the advent of the use of computer-generated imagery (or CGI) in films, film-makers struggled to convey the sheer size of the Second Temple in Jerusalem, which had nevertheless to be represented in some way in most films about Jesus. In *The Greatest Story Ever Told*, the Temple set consists of little more than the Court of the Priests with a shallow colonnade around its edge. The tables of the money-changers which Max von Sydow as Jesus overturns are located inside this colonnade, and there is easy access to the altar and the front of the inner sanctum. Here Jesus even preaches a long sermon to a mixed crowd of men and women, few of whom appear to be priests, as he stands on the altar itself. Later Judas, played by David McCallum, kills himself by falling into the fire that burns on the altar. The entire set is made of a uniform grey fake stone, with no sign of the gleaming white and gold that visitors so admired.

3. The Burden of Power

As High Priest Caiaphas went about his duties in the Temple, and perhaps looked up at it from his palace in the city, it must at times have seemed permanent and unassailable. Any feelings of this kind that Caiaphas and his fellow priests entertained would, however, have been without firm foundations. As we have seen, the Temple was not always a place that everybody considered to be so sacred and important that it was allowed to continue with its holy work unchallenged, and the high priest of the place had regularly to face up to threats and challenges from many different directions.

By far the greatest risk to the Temple, and to Jerusalem and the whole Jewish way of life in Caiaphas's time, came from the Romans. It was, after all, a Roman who had found a way to enter into the Holy of Holies without being dragged out and killed, as had nearly happened to Paul merely because of a vague suspicion that he might have been responsible for introducing a Gentile into one of the inner courts of the Temple. In 63 BCE the Roman leader Pompey the Great laid siege to part of Jerusalem for three months, using the whole panoply of Roman techniques including siege engines, siege towers and battering-rams. Josephus tells us that the Temple priests continued their sacrifices throughout this siege as if nothing was happening, even though flying darts and rocks thrown by ballistas (giant catapults) were taking their toll. At last the Romans broke into the Temple and massacred some twelve thousand Jews, some of whom were priests who were cut down while they were still going about their priestly duties, as Josephus tells us in his *Jewish War*:

And now did many of the priests, even when they saw their enemies assailing them with swords in their hands, without any disturbance, go on with their Divine worship, and were slain while they were offering their drink-offerings, and burning their incense, as preferring the duties about their worship to God before their own preservation.

(trans. Whiston)

It was then that Pompey the great committed the terrible sacrilege of entering the Holy of Holies, but he secured the Temple without taking away its many treasures, including its gold decorations and furniture, heaps of precious spices and 'two thousand talents of sacred money'.

Pompey's invasion in 63 BCE had been prompted by a conflict between two brothers, both leading members of the then ruling Jewish Hasmonean dynasty; Hyrcanus II and Aristobulus II. It was Hyrcanus II who later lost his ears to his nephew, the son of Aristobulus II. The second Hyrcanus was interesting not least because he reigned briefly as both high priest and king of the Jews.

One Herod Antipater was chief advisor to Hycanus II during this conflict, and this man was to go on to found the famous dynasty of the Herods which succeeded the Hasmoneans as rulers of the area. Herod the Great was a son of Antipater, and his own son Archelaus ruled Judea for a time as a puppet of the Romans.

After the downfall of Herod Archelaus in 6 CE, Judea, together with Samaria and Idumea, came under the control of a series of Roman prefects. Archelaus's father Herod the Great had been a puppet ruler of much of the region for the Romans, and as such it was he who ordered the executions of the young men who had hacked the Roman eagle from the entrance to the Temple, as detailed above. Herod's rough justice also extended to two of the rabbis who had inspired this anti-Roman act, which was also a criticism of his own decision to put the eagle there in the first place. Soon after Herod the Great died, these forty-two executions led to a noisy, potentially dangerous demonstration of public grief in the Temple, and as things escalated Herod's son Archelaus sent in troops and massacred perhaps three thousand people.

Having thus impressed the locals with his ruthlessness, Archelaus hot-footed it to Rome to have his position as ruler of Judea confirmed by the emperor Augustus. Despite the opposition of members of his own family, Archelaus was indeed confirmed as 'ethnarch' of Judea and other areas, but his continued cruelty, and his controversial marriage to his sister-in-law Glaphyra, led to pressure for his removal. At last Augustus had Archelaus banished to Vienne in France, and appointed the first of a series of Roman prefects to the area.

Both Pompey's successful siege of Jerusalem in 63 BCE and the removal of Herod Archelaus in 6 CE were examples of classic imperialist divide-and-rule tactics from the Romans. The first, as we have seen, took advantage of a family feud within the Hasmonean dynasty, and the second exploited similar tensions among the Herodians, and between the Herodians and their Jewish subjects. As Idumeans, from the country the Bible sometimes calls Edom, the Herods were regarded with suspicion by many Jews, although they were technically Jews by religion. After 6 CE, the Temple priests and other Judean locals who were Jewish both by religion and ethnicity had to reckon with a European ruler, appointed by a distant emperor, a prefect who was frankly Pagan and probably had no roots in, or personal commitment to, Judea at all.

While the Romans dominated the area, the local rulers, representatives of the Temple priests and others often found it expedient to travel to Rome, as Archelaus had done. There they would petition for political, financial or military aid and advice, answer accusations, accuse their enemies, seek asylum and, as in Archelaus' case, seek confirmation of their exact position vis-a-vis the empire. It was understood that lavish gifts handed over to key Roman figures, accompanied by over-the-top compliments, were considered appropriate, and it must have helped to be able to claim that one had, for example, erected a temple or held games in honour of a member of the Roman imperial family, back in Judea.

At times, the business of going cap-in-hand to the Eternal City must have made the Jews and Idumeans feel a little like school-children who have to stand on the carpet in front of the head-teacher's desk to explain their actions. Even when important Roman officials such as the Governor of Syria visited Judea, they might be called upon to adjudicate in disputes between the locals, hire and fire local officials, and agree to adjustments in the political and financial settlement between the Judeans and the occupying power.

The Roman governors of Judea, who are often referred to as 'procurators', though they were not given that title until some time after the crucifixion of Jesus, were drawn from the equestrian or knightly class, and knew themselves to be inferior to the more important Roman governors of Syria. It was probably the fourth of these Judean governors, a man called Valerius Gratus, who deposed Caiaphas's father-in-law Annas as high priest of the Temple and replaced him with a succession of three high priests over the next three years. At last, perhaps in 18 CE, Valerius appointed Joseph Caiaphas, a son-in-law of Annas, to the high priesthood. Caiaphas remained as high priest for another eighteen years or so, until he in turn was deposed, not by a Roman governor of Judea, but by Lucius Vitellius, who was then governor of Syria.

Their Roman rulers had inherited the power of deposing high priests from their predecessors as rulers of Judea – the Herods. This power, which Valerius Gratus in particular seemed to enjoy exercising, sits oddly beside the fact that as Gentiles and Pagans, most Romans could only penetrate as far as the Temple's Court of the Gentiles, and may have had problems understanding the significance of the Temple and its high priests, and the duties of the latter.

Readers who have seen one or more of the films of *Ben-Hur*, or read the 1880 novel of the same name by Lew Wallace, may remember that it is Valerius Gratus, the Roman governor of Judea who appointed Caiaphas, who is nearly killed when the eponymous hero accidentally knocks a roof-tile onto his head. This is the incident that leads to Ben-Hur's subsequent troubles and adventures.

Caiaphas had been high priest of the Jerusalem Temple for around eight years when Valerius Gratus was replaced by a new governor, Pontius Pilate. It is possible that Caiaphas retained his office for so long because the Romans found it easy to get on with him. Conversely, his predecessors in the post may have caused the Roman authorities too many problems, assembled too much power to themselves, or failed to respond adequately to the various threats that both the Romans and the Temple priesthood had to face together.

Roughly ten of Caiaphas's eighteen years as high priest were spent in co-existence with the most famous (or notorious) of all the Roman governors of Judea – Pontius Pilate. Earlier high priests might have expected to put up with their Roman governors for a far shorter period, but it was the policy of the second Roman emperor, Tiberius, to keep such officials in office for as long as possible. When asked about this, Tiberius explained that new provincial governors tended to extract as much wealth from their respective provinces as they possibly could in their first years, so by keeping a man on for several more years, a few years of proper rule rather than just asset-stripping might be more likely to happen.

Although Caiaphas remained in office throughout Pilate's time as governor of Judea, some of the latter's actions placed a severe strain on Jewish-Roman relations. As is related in more detail in my book *What Do We Know About Pontius Pilate?*, it is difficult to link the dates when any of these things happened to events in the gospels, or to specific years during Pilate's tenure in Judea, but they do give an insight into the nature of the man and the kinds of problems that beset Caiaphas and his people at the time.

According to Josephus, Pilate committed the *faux pas* of marching soldiers into the Jewish holy city of Jerusalem carrying banners bearing images that offended the traditional Jewish ban on depictions of people or gods. A crowd of local people went to protest about this to Pilate at his usual place of residence, the seaside city of Caesarea Maritima. The governor appeared to the crowd, and when they would not listen to him, the soldiers he had concealed nearby emerged, and Pilate threatened to have the people killed. Pilate was very impressed when the Jews cried that they would rather die than see their holy city contaminated. At last, Pilate agreed to remove the standards back to Caesarea, a more westernised, Hellenistic city with a diverse population, where such Pagan symbols would cause less offence.

Some offensive plaques that Pilate had had installed in his Jerusalem house, which had probably been a palace of Herod the Great, also had to be removed to Caesarea, this time on the orders of the emperor Tiberius, who had probably appointed Pilate in the first place.

When Pilate built an aqueduct to bring water to Jerusalem, he made the mistake of appropriating funds from the holy 'corban' money of the Temple to pay for it. This resulted in another protest, but Pilate had concealed armed men in the crowd who started to lash out at the protesters at a given signal. It seems that his men got carried away, exceeded their orders, attacked protesters and bystanders alike, and many were killed and injured, some in the stampede to escape.

The accounts of Pilate's oppressive actions, as described above, in both Josephus and the works of the Jewish philosopher Philo of Alexandria, do not mention any involvement by Caiaphas, though surely he must have been aware of these events. Pilate's use of money from the Temple could hardly have happened without Caiaphas being informed, but no response from him is recorded – or is it? Could it be that he was ultimately responsible for the protests against these actions, both in the form of concerned and orderly petitions, like the one recorded by Philo of Alexandria concerning the plaques, and the more threatening mass protests. Was Caiaphas a rabble-rouser? There may be evidence that he was in both the gospels and the Book of Acts.

As well as the very real threats to Caiaphas's power that came from the Romans, his own Jewish people must also have given him cause for concern at times. The Jews of the Holy Land, and those who lived elsewhere, in the so-called diaspora, were certainly not the type of homogeneous group that is easy to manage. As well as the usual class, caste, financial, vocational, educational and geographical divisions, the Jews even took different approaches to their religion: in his *Jewish War*, Josephus tells us about three distinct sects that divided Judaism at this time.

The first, to which Josephus devotes the most room, are the Essenes. These men lived as some orders of medieval Christian monks lived, remaining celibate and keeping themselves to themselves in other ways. They shared everything in common, so that new members gave all their wealth to the community as a whole, which meant that, according to Josephus (who evidently admired the Essenes) there was no excessive wealth, poverty or inequality to be found among them. They all dressed the same, lived a life of prayer and devotion, and some Essene groups secured their survival into the next generation by adopting boys who seemed suited to their way of life. This makes them similar not only to medieval Christian monks, but also to the Shakers of nineteenth-century America, who were celibate, but ran orphanages from which the next generation of Shakers were drawn.

Other Essenes practised marriage and fathered children, but their wives, it seems, were kept strictly for breeding purposes. Once the woman was pregnant, all sex would stop and man and wife would live separately again.

Because of their distinctive way of life, and their desire to avoid the temptations and contaminations of the world, the Essenes kept themselves very much to themselves, and Jerusalem and other cities had Essene areas or enclaves. Although they sent offerings to the Temple, they made their own sacrifices elsewhere. They seem not to have been a threat to mainstream Judaism or the institutions of the Temple, but their ascetic way of life could have been seen as an implicit criticism of the wealth and worldliness of the Jewish aristocracy of the time, from whose ranks the high priests were drawn.

The Essenes are long gone, but the next Jewish sect of Jesus' time, the Pharisees, are said to have formed the foundation of modern Rabbinical Judaism. The Pharisees followed the Torah, the law and definition of Judaism as contained in the first five books of what Christians call the Old Testament, but they also believed that the oral traditions that had been passed on via the generations of Jewish people were important. These traditions were later codified as the Mishnah, an important part of the Talmud, a vast and indispensable compilation of Jewish teachings.

By taking into account the oral tradition, the Pharisees were adding to the law, which made them unpopular with the next sect, the Sadducees, although Josephus, who was probably a Pharisee himself, tells us that the Pharisees were popular among the Jewish people in general.

St Paul claimed to be a Pharisee, and indeed certain beliefs of the Pharisees are more consistent with Christianity than some of the beliefs of the third sect, the Sadducees. In particular, the Sadducees' refusal to accept the idea of the immortality of the soul set them apart from Jesus, Paul and the first Christians, and made their view of the universe different from most religious groups, both ancient and modern. These have a strong tendency to believe in the persistence of something like a soul, whether through reincarnation in a later generation of humans or animals, or in the heaven or hell that await the just and the unjust respectively. It seems that many Jews at the time of Jesus believed that the virtuous dead would be resurrected, as both Lazarus and Jesus himself were. As we have seen, the gospel of Matthew tells us that many other holy people rose from their tombs and walked into Jerusalem at the time of Jesus' death on the cross (Matt 27: 52). Many modern faiths also continue to believe in angels and spirits, which the Sadducees rejected.

According to the gospels of Matthew, Mark and Luke, a group of Sadducees tried to trick Jesus into admitting the absurdity of the idea of the resurrection of the dead by presenting him with the case of a woman who had married seven brothers in turn, all of whom died. 'At the resurrection whose wife will she be,' asked the Sadducees, 'since the seven were married to her?' (Mk 12: 23)

Jesus explained that there was no marriage among the resurrected ones, who lived like the angels in heaven. He also pointed out that when God spoke to Moses out of the burning bush, he said that he was the god of Abraham, Isaac and Jacob. Since God is the God of the living and not of the dead, then surely those earlier figures must still be alive? (Mk 12: 26-7)

Although, like the Essenes, the Sadducees are now long

gone, they were very influential at the time of Jesus, and they were also the dominant sect among the Jewish aristocracy and the Temple priesthood. They placed a greater emphasis on the importance of the Temple and of priestly rites, rights, authority and privileges than the other sects, and it is thought that Caiaphas himself may have been a Sadducee. At Acts 5:17 we learn that the high priest and his associates were Sadducees, but Luke, who is widely regarded as the author of Acts, seems to be under the impression that Annas, Caiaphas's father-in-law, was high priest at this time, when the Temple authorities threw Peter and the apostles in prison for daring to preach their new message in the Court of the Gentiles. Annas is supposed to have been deposed over a decade earlier, so it is unclear to whom Luke is referring here.

4. Threats

In his *Jewish War*, Josephus names three main Jewish sects in the passage where he takes a few pages to describe and explain these groups. In his *Antiquities of the Jews*, he names a fourth sect, the members of which were, according to the historian, devotees of the theological ideas of the Pharisees. What distinguished the Zealots from the other three sects was not so much their belief system as their rather more direct approach. Whereas the Essenes lived like monks, the Sadducees looked after the Temple, and the Pharisees passed on the faith of the people, the Zealots embraced violent revolt as a means of expressing, and indeed imposing, their beliefs.

According to Josephus, the founders of this dangerous fourth sect were one Judas the Galilean and a Pharisee called Sadduc. The immediate cause of the revolt was the so-called census of Quirinius, which happened in 6 CE, after the fall of Archelaus. As part of the Romans' imposition of direct rule on Judea at this time, Quirinius, governor of Syria, was ordered to begin this 'census', which was an attempt to impose a kind of poll tax on the local people. Quirinius and his census are mentioned in the gospel of Luke (2: 1-5) where we learn that the census happened at the time of the birth of Jesus: to pay his taxes, Joseph was forced to return to Bethlehem with his heavily-pregnant wife. Commentators have long suspected that Luke made a mistake here, as he places the census during the reign of Herod the Great, who had died some years earlier.

While Joseph was supposed to have literally gone out of his way to pay Quirinius's tax, Judas the Galilean and his like-minded followers refused to do so, seeing it as a way of enslaving the Jews. They started over sixty years of violent resistance to the Romans and those who collaborated with them: at last this led to the disastrous Jewish War against the Romans of which Josephus writes, and in which the historian himself played a leading part.

One branch of the Zealots comprised the *sicarii*, or dagger-men, who went about with concealed knives and stabbed their opponents. Some believe that St Paul, when he was still called Saul, was a Zealot with Pharisaic sympathies, who persecuted the earliest Christians because he believed that their doctrines were a threat to the Jewish faith. In the 1988 film *The Last Temptation of Christ* Saul, played by Harry Dean Stanton, is even depicted as one of the *sicarii*, who stabs Jesus' friend Lazarus because the continued life of this resurrected man proves that Jesus has miraculous powers. There is justification for this idea in the New Testament – at John 12:10 we learn that the Jewish hierarchy were planning to kill Lazarus.

We have possible evidence of Zealots in Jerusalem during the last days before the crucifixion of Jesus. Again in Luke (13: 1-5) Jesus is told that a number of Galileans have been killed by Pontius Pilate, the Roman governor of Judea, in such a way that their own blood was mingled with the blood of their sacrifices. This has been taken to mean that, while some Galileans were sacrificing Passover lambs in the Temple, agents of Pilate stormed in and killed them. This incident probably happened during the Passover festival, as this was the only time when ordinary Jews, for instance from Galilee, could make their own sacrifices: at other times of the year, only priests could do this.

The men Pilate had killed in this way could easily have

been Zealots – as we have seen, this ancient terrorist group began in Galilee and was always associated with that area, where the landscape made it easier for fugitives to hide away. What these men had done to offend Pilate is unclear – commenting on their case, Jesus remarks that the men who were killed in the Temple were no more guilty that any other Galileans – the manner of their deaths was not a result of their sin. He compares their fates and their standing with God with some other men who were accidentally killed nearby when a tower collapsed – the nature of these men's deaths had not been brought on them by their guilt. But, Jesus asserts, death will come to those who do not repent. He then goes on to give the example of the owner of a vineyard who is tempted to cut down a fig tree that has not borne fruit for three years. He is advised to wait another year after fertiliser is put around the tree: if it still does not produce figs, then it should be pulled up and burned. Here Jesus is saying that the time for repentance is now, but God can be patient – up to a point.

In Luke, Jesus hears about the murders in the Temple some time before his triumphal entry into Jerusalem on what we call Palm Sunday. That he is able to hear news from Jerusalem suggests, of course, that by the same token people in Jerusalem were able to hear news about him, and, given the nature of some of Jesus' actions, and of his preaching at this time, Jerusalem-based figures like Caiaphas may not have been entirely happy with what they heard. Shortly after Jesus hears news of the Temple murders in Luke, he is invited to the house of a Pharisee, and we are told that his actions at a Sabbath dinner there are being carefully watched. He performs a miraculous cure at this gathering, of a man who was probably suffering from dropsy. For whom were the other guests 'watching' Jesus? Did news of the healing miracle and of Jesus' subsequent preaching reach the ears of Caiaphas?

At the banquet, Jesus tells a story of a man who prepares

just such a banquet, and invites all his friends, who all, however, make excuses and fail to come. So the frustrated host sends his servant out into the streets to invite 'the poor, the crippled, the blind and the lame' (Lk 14:21). Jesus tells this story in response to a pious declaration from one of the other guests: 'Blessed is the one who will eat at the feast in the kingdom of God' (Lk 14:15). Given the context, this story could be perceived as a direct criticism of the Jewish elite, who are too busy to come to God's feast. But there will be room for the poor, and for 'the crippled, the blind and the lame' who would not then have been allowed to sacrifice at the main Temple altar, or to enter into the ante-room of the Holy of Holies, even if they were priests.

Still following Luke, we find that soon after Jesus' reaction to the news of the Temple murders, he is healing a crippled woman in a synagogue on the Sabbath. When the leader of the synagogue objects to this, Jesus calls him a hypocrite. Later, when some Pharisees warn Jesus that Herod Antipas is determined to kill him, he hints at his determination to come to Jerusalem itself, at all costs.

If Caiaphas was hearing news about Jesus' activities at this time, he would not only have heard about miraculous cures and challenging parables, but also of large crowds following Jesus around, and of his willingness to preach to sinners and tax-collectors. The famous parallel of the Prodigal Son is even told in response to some Pharisees' objection to the 'lost' whom Jesus, it seems, was trying to recover. From Caiaphas' palace in Jerusalem this may have sounded like an attempt by a popular preacher to gather support from hitherto neglected quarters.

Other stories told by Jesus at this time hint at the punishments in store for misers and people who do not manage other people's wealth wisely. At Luke 16:14-15 we are reminded that the Pharisees love money, which suggests that Jesus' warnings about the worthlessness of wealth are aimed at them.

Not content with relying on gossip and other people's spies to spread news of his preaching and other activities, Luke tells us that when Jesus encounters ten lepers, he instructs them to go and tell the priests that they are cured: they all shed their dreaded disease on the way. Jesus declares that the best of these is a Samaritan, a member of a distinct ethnic and religious group whom the Jews were supposed to despise. Only the Samaritan leper comes back to thank Jesus for his cure.

If Caiaphas was reading reports about all this in his Jerusalem palace or in some office in the Temple complex, one can imagine him grinding his teeth in consternation. Did he begin to have visions of a vast army of thousands of beggars, cripples, lepers, Samaritans, outcasts, sinners and tax-collectors descending on Jerusalem with Jesus at their head, to stir up trouble?

At Luke 17-25 Jesus warns that the coming of his kingdom – the coming of the Son of Man – will be like Noah's flood, or the destruction of Sodom and Gomorrah. Could a man with such a huge investment in the *status quo* as Caiaphas take such a message calmly? In other utterances from this time, Jesus criticises the rich, the proud and the self-righteous, and promises justice for those who have longed for justice in vain.

In his story of the rich man and Lazarus (Lk 16:19-31) Jesus tells us about a man who callously neglects to feed or otherwise help Lazarus, a sick beggar at his gate. When both men die, Lazarus ascends to heaven and sits with Abraham, while the rich man is tormented in hell. Such a story may have offended Caiaphas, not only because he was rich, but also because, as a Sadducee, he did not believe in any kind of afterlife.

In Luke's account of the time immediately before Jesus' Palm Sunday entry into Jerusalem, it is often Pharisees who criticise the Galilean, while also keeping a careful watch over him. When Jesus' entry starts to look like the arrival of a king, with much cheering and rejoicing, it is a group of Pharisees in the crowd who suggest that Jesus should tell his followers to take it down a notch (Lk 19:39).

The fact that Jesus chose the time of the Passover festival to enter Jerusalem in this way was probably seen by Caiaphas and others in the Jewish, Roman and Herodian hierarchy as a deliberate provocation. At this time, the city was usually full to bursting, with people sleeping in the streets and on roof-tops, and even on the hills outside the walls. It was a time when trouble and even violence could break out. As a result, the Roman governor, at this time Pontius Pilate, usually spent Passover in Jerusalem, instead of at his usual seat, the seaside city of Caesarea. Luke tells us that Herod Antipas was also in Jerusalem for this particular Passover: this is why it is possible for Pontius Pilate to send Jesus to Herod (Lk 23:7-15), an episode which is not included in the other gospels.

Directly after his entry into the city, Luke tells us that Jesus weeps openly for Jerusalem and predicts its total destruction (Lk 19:41-44). As we have seen, when he first enters the Temple, he casts out the merchants who are trading there, citing two Old Testament prophets, Isaiah and Jeremiah, to justify his actions (Lk 19:45-46). Luke's account of this event is very short: it merely states that Jesus drove out people who were selling things there, and does not even say what they were selling. Mark, by contrast, has a fuller account, saying that Jesus drove out both the people who were selling and those who were buying. Mark also mentions that doves were being sold, and that Jesus overturned the tables of the money-changers. Also according to Mark, Jesus forbade people to carry merchandise through the Temple. John adds more details, saying that Jesus made an impromptu whip out of chords and with it drove out the sellers of sheep and cattle, then turned on the sellers of doves and told them to leave.

In Matthew, Mark and Luke, this so-called 'cleansing of

the temple' causes official alarm and hostility about Jesus to escalate. In these so-called synoptic gospels the cleansing is soon followed by the attempts of those in authority in Jerusalem to capture and kill Jesus. In John, the cleansing is placed surprisingly early in the gospel: it is an incident that takes place during one of a series of visits Jesus and his disciples make to Jerusalem and its Temple.

In none of the accounts are we told that Jesus actually drove out the money-changers, only that he overturned their tables and scattered their coins. These people served a vital function: they changed the Roman or other coins devotees brought to the Temple into the Jewish or Tyrian coins that were actually accepted by the Temple authorities. It may be that as the merchants and their livestock were being driven out, the tables of the money-changers were accidentally overturned.

In his 1968 book *The Trial of Jesus of Nazareth*, S.G.F. Brandon suggests that Jesus' cleansing of the Temple was a much bigger and more alarming event than some commentators have imagined. Brandon implies that to have driven out these traders, Jesus must have had a large group of supporters with him, otherwise the traders and the Temple police would surely have resisted. If, as Mark tells us, Jesus also prevented people from carrying merchandise through the Temple precincts, then we should not think of the cleansing of the Temple in the way it is often depicted in paintings and on screen – as a one-off, short-lived demonstration where Jesus stands as a solitary, active, righteous figure. This was more like a large, intimidating demonstration by a considerable number of well-motivated people, commanded and coordinated in some way by the figure of Jesus.

Brandon notes that the reaction of the Temple authorities to this event shows that they were truly rattled. Mark tells us that as soon as they heard about it, 'the chief priests and the teachers of the law . . . began looking for a way to kill'

Jesus. That they did not feel able to act immediately is explained by the fact that they feared Jesus, and the crowds that followed his teaching.

The effects of Jesus' cleansing of the Temple are clear, but his reasons for the cleansing are less obvious. Brandon suggests that Jesus attempted to cleanse the Temple in this way because he wanted to expose and challenge the hierarchy of the Temple itself. I am in charge now, he was saying – from now on, I make the rules. In an important article published in 1964, Victor Eppstein argued that Jesus' attack may have been intended less as a scatter-gun blast of criticism aimed at the Temple hierarchy in general, but rather as a more focused shot intended specifically for Caiaphas himself. Eppstein maintains that Jesus objected to the presence of the merchants and their wares in the Temple precincts partly because they had only recently been allowed to start trading there, thanks to a change made by the high priest.

Whether Jesus was objecting to a new innovation that seemed to him to be cheapening the role of the Temple, or whether he intended this protest as a specific attack on the high priest and his associates, the fact that he succeeded in driving out the merchants, if only temporarily, and that he felt that he had the right and the authority to do so, must have got the attention of the people in charge. The fact that he also somehow managed to slip away and avoid capture at this time may also have seemed particularly alarming to the Temple hierarchy. Perhaps, as Brandon suggests, the crowd that surrounded Jesus, and may have helped him drive out the merchants, also made it impossible for the Temple police to make an arrest.

Unable to use strong-arm tactics on Jesus during his public appearances in Jerusalem at this time, Matthew, Mark and Luke agree that the chief priests, scribes and elders braved the crowds and attempted to probe any cracks in Jesus' theological armour by asking him what they evidently thought were tricky questions. Jesus refused to answer the first question, about the source of his authority, until his questioners had answered a question of his – where did John the Baptist get his authority? He then preached the parable of the wicked tenants (Mk 12:1-12) which the members of the Temple hierarchy understood to be directed against them: in this story, they are cast as the greedy, dishonest tenants of a vineyard owned by another man, who try to avoid their responsibilities to the owner. Jesus, they were to understand, was the son of the owner (meaning God himself) whom they killed. God was the owner who would return to destroy them, the criminal tenants.

The next set of people who fail to trap Jesus with his own words include Pharisees and also 'Herodians', people who backed the collaborationist, westernising approach of the Herodian dynasty. They asked Jesus if it was lawful to pay taxes to the Romans, and Jesus gave his famous reply about rendering unto Caesar that which is Caesar's. Next came the Sadducees, who set Jesus the aforementioned puzzle about the woman who had married, and been widowed by, seven brothers in succession. Who would be her husband in the afterlife?

In the succeeding days, Jesus continued to preach in ways that could be interpreted as critical of the *status quo* in Jerusalem. He employed parables to do this, such as the parable of the wicked tenants mentioned above, and, in Matthew, the parable of the two sons (Matt 21:28-32). Jesus ended this parable with the message that even tax collectors and prostitutes would go into the kingdom of God before the chief priests and the elders, because they had believed in John the Baptist and his message.

There seems little doubt that the parables of Jesus were one reason why he was such a hit with the people. Delivered, no doubt, in an accessible form of Aramaic, Jesus' own mother tongue, or in street or Koine Greek for Gentiles, they were engaging, memorable and easy to interpret. They were also well-adapted to the issues Jesus was trying to address, in much the same way that Jesus' miracles at this time could be taken as symbols of his larger goals. As versions of these stories and miracles spread outwards like ripples in a pond, it seems that the new motion in the water was making those in authority in Jerusalem distinctly queasy.

As well as parables and miracles, Jesus was also making prophecies about his own death, the destruction of the Temple, and about more general changes in the nature of the world as a whole. For those who were more than content with things as they were, these prophecies could not but be alarming. Little did they know that by trying to silence the prophet, they were merely helping to turn his prophecies into reality.

5. Action

A writer who set himself the task of producing a novel with Caiaphas as the central character might be tempted to show the high priest personally sending out people to spy on Jesus, and others to confound him with awkward questions. The novelist might also show Caiaphas pumping his spies for information and, when the gospels say 'the high priests' went to visit Jesus where he preached in the Temple, perhaps the fictionalised Caiaphas would confront the Galilean preacher in person before his trial in front of the Sanhedrin, when it is usually assumed that the two men first met face to face. Unfortunately, we do not have enough information on Caiaphas's activities at this time to be able to tell how deeply he was involved, and how early in the story he *became* involved – in fact we have very little direct information about the man at all.

The gospels often hint at groups within the Jewish hierarchy plotting against Jesus and his followers, but until Caiaphas steps onto the stage after Jesus' arrest, his role is unclear, at least in Matthew, Mark and Luke. In John, we are told that, in direct response to the publicity surrounding the resurrection of Lazarus, the Sanhedrin held a meeting to determine what to do about Jesus (Jn 11:47-53). At this meeting, the Sanhedrin in general are supposed to have said, 'If we let him go on like this, everyone will believe in him, and then the Romans will come and take away both our temple and our nation' (Jn 11:48). In response Caiaphas said that it would be better for one man 'to die for the people than that the whole nation perish' (Jn 11:50). Here John comments that Caiaphas was inadvertently prophesying that 'Jesus would die for the Jewish nation, and not only for that nation but also for the scattered children of God, to bring them together and make them one' (Jn 11:51-2). The gospel of John is, however, thought to be further from the original Jesus stories than the other gospels, and it is possible that Caiaphas's intervention in the alleged meeting of the Sanhedrin is merely an elaboration of John's.

While John places Caiaphas in a meeting that might be described as part of a plot against Jesus, the other gospels refer more vaguely to the actions and intentions of various groups including 'the high priests'. It is entirely believable that these gospel writers remained unaware of the specifics of any plots against Jesus, especially if they were drawing on their own reminiscences as early followers of the Galilean, or on such memories inherited from an earlier generation. When Jesus was approached by a group of people trying to confound him with a question, about the afterlife and a woman who had been widowed by seven brothers, it is likely that Jesus and the disciples would have been able to recognise these men as Sadducees, but how could they know who had sent them, or if they had not been sent by anybody at all, but had merely decided to try to confound Jesus among themselves?

If the Sadducees involved had been sent by Caiaphas, they would not be likely to admit that they had just come straight from the high priest. They would perhaps have tried to create the impression that they were just disinterested questioners, curious about Jesus' opinions on their own account.

When the gospels mention 'the high priests' it is often unclear exactly who they can mean. There was only one high priest at a time: could the term 'high priests' be referring to a group of men near the top of the Temple hierarchy? If the gospels used 'high priest', singular, instead, we would surely have to assume that they meant Caiaphas. Or was Caiaphas's father-in-law, the deposed high priest Annas, still so powerful that the gospel writers thought that there were two high priests at this time?

The continued power of Annas might have been another factor that compromised Caiaphas's personal power and his freedom of action. As well as the Romans and the Herods, Caiaphas had to contend with the different factions and sects among the Jews; and closer to home his father-in-law had perhaps continued to hang on to parts of the power Caiaphas himself should have enjoyed.

It may be that Annas's position was similar to that of the much-respected veteran head of a large company, who is forced to step down as CEO when then firm falls victim to a hostile takeover. But the old CEO still owns a lot of shares, continues to sit on the board, gives TV interviews and entertains important clients at his luxury mansion, and, although he is supposed to be semi-retired, is still seen around company headquarters pretty much every day. In this analogy, the larger concern that swallows up Temple Inc. is the Rome Corporation.

According to the synoptic gospels of Matthew, Mark and Luke, the chief priests (whoever they were), the scribes, the elders and even the Herodians tested Jesus' ideas, trying to find traces of error, or heresy, or sedition against the Romans but, according to the gospels, they all failed miserably. Open arrest was impossible in the day-time, while Jesus was surrounded by hundreds of listeners in the Temple. But where did he go at night? How many were with him then? Who knew the answer? Were all his followers as unshakeable as his own message? Could not one of them be persuaded to betray him, and lead a hostile force to him at a vulnerable time, to spirit him away without too many of the people knowing?

According to John, splits began to appear six days before Jesus' last Passover festival, when the Galilean and his disciples were having supper in the house of Lazarus, whom Jesus had raised from the dead, and his sisters Mary and Martha (Jn 12:1-8). Mary begins to anoint Jesus with spikenard, a precious essential oil, and Judas Iscariot objects and says that the oil could have been sold for three hundred dinarii and the money given to the poor. At this point in John, the narrator breaks in and suggests that this was sheer hypocrisy on Judas's part: it was he who kept the bag of money for the disciples, and he stole out of it. The poor, John implies, would have seen nothing of any three hundred dinarii. Responding to Judas's words, Jesus suggests that Mary keep the rest of the oil to anoint his dead body.

The story of the so-called anointing at Bethany is radically different in Matthew, Mark and Luke. In Matthew and Mark, Jesus and the disciples are not dining with Lazarus and his sisters at all, but with one Simon the leper. In Luke, Simon is identified as a Pharisee, and it is the host, not Judas, who objects to the anointing because the woman, who is not named in the synoptic gospels, is a sinner. In Matthew and Mark, the disciples in general object to the use of the oil, saying that the cost of it could have been given to the poor.

None of the gospels identify the woman who does the anointing as Mary Magdalen, though in many dramatic representations of this scene it is she who is shown doing the anointing. In paintings, Mary can often be identified by the flask of oil that is her attribute, in the same way that keys are attributed to St Peter, and a sword to St Paul.

Although in these gospels Judas Iscariot is not identified as the sole objector to the alleged waste of the expensive oil, in Matthew and Mark the anointing at Bethany is immediately followed by Judas's visit to 'the chief priests', where the betrayer promises to deliver Jesus into their

117

hands. In Matthew, they give him the famous thirty pieces of silver, whereas in Mark and Luke they merely promise to give him an unspecified amount of money (Mt 26:15).

In screen adaptations of the Passion, Caiaphas and sometimes his father-in-law Annas are shown conspiring with Judas at this time, but again we cannot be sure exactly what the gospels mean by 'the high priests' here. In Mel Gibson's controversial 2004 film *The Passion of the Christ*, a large group of priests in which Caiaphas and Annas are prominent give Judas his silver; but the question remains, would Caiaphas, as sole high priest himself, really have condescended to take part in such sordid deals – was he really that 'hands on'?

The deal with Judas allows an armed group sent by 'the chief priests' to take Jesus at night when only a few followers are with him. In Matthew, Mark and John the group is understood to have been sent not only by the chief priests but also by 'the elders of the people' (Matthew), by 'the scribes and elders' (Mark) and by 'the Pharisees' (John). The language used in John suggests that the group was made up of soldiers and officers, though the composition of the group is left completely vague in Luke.

Here as elsewhere, the reader of this part of the New Testament gospels gets the impression of a vague group of Jewish priests and others in authority plotting to capture Jesus. This impression, which tends to make Caiaphas in particular seem like a rather blurred, shadowy character, is strengthened by the fact that Caiaphas is not mentioned by name at all in the gospel of Mark, and in Luke is merely named, early on in the book, as one of the two high priests (the other is of course Annas) during whose term of office the word of God came to John the Baptist (Lk 3:2). The character and role of Caiaphas, and the extent of his influence, is also rendered unclear by the frequent mentions of Annas in the gospels. Could they really have shared the high priestly office? Did they take it in turns, or, as is more likely, did Annas, like the semi-retired CEO mentioned above, exercise so much power from his semi-retirement that his son-in-law Caiaphas was merely his puppet?

Certainly the other two main sources of power in the Holy Land at this time – the Romans and the Herodian family – seem not to be involved in the Jesus problem at all at the time of his arrest. That Herod Antipas is out of the picture is hardly surprising – Antipas's areas of influence did not include Judea, where Jerusalem was situated. It may be that, though he was probably not directly involved at this point, the Roman governor of Judea, Pontius Pilate, was aware of the 'Jesus problem', but viewed it as a purely Jewish matter.

One of the structural problems with the sprawling 1965 Biblical film *The Greatest Story Ever Told*, some prints of which stretch to over four hours, is that Antipas, played by Jose Ferrer, Pilate (Telly Savalas), and Martin Landau's Caiaphas are all determined to capture Jesus, and silence his preaching, from fairly early on in the action. This confuses the all-important element of conflict in the film – who is the enemy?

In Matthew, Jesus, now under arrest, is led straight to 'Caiaphas the high priest' (Mt 26:57). Some English translations add 'the house of' here, before Caiaphas's name, but the location of the subsequent events is not definitely stated until we learn that Peter, who will soon deny his link to Jesus three times, has followed Jesus and his captors, at a distance, into 'the court of the high priest' (Mt 26:58).

Confusingly, John tells us that Jesus is taken first to Annas, who then sends him to Caiaphas, and because the terms 'high priest' and 'high priests' are used in descriptions of these events in all four gospels, it is sometimes hard to determine who said what, and when. Even the identity of the owner of the house, palace, court or courtyard where Jesus was interrogated by the senior Jews has been called into question. If, as John states, Jesus was first taken to Annas, were Annas and Caiaphas living in the same house, did Annas send Jesus across town to the house of Caiaphas, was he, Annas, already at Caiaphas's house, or did Caiaphas come to his, Annas's, house?

In Matthew, a high priest, who seems, by the context, to be Caiaphas, listens with 'the chief priests and the whole council' while an unspecified number of witnesses give their evidence. There seems to be no evidence given, either true or false, that speaks to any crime committed by Jesus, until two men testify that Jesus had said he could destroy the Temple, and re-build it in three days (Mt 26:61). According to John, Jesus had indeed said this, as he preached in the Temple just after he had driven out the merchants (Jn 2:19), but John explains to us that Jesus had meant *the temple of his body*, that would live again after three days in the tomb.

Seizing, it would seem, on something that sounded like it could incriminate the prisoner, the high priest challenged Jesus, asking him to answer the charge, or at least give his interpretation of it. When Jesus responded with silence, the high priest asked him directly, by the name of the living God, if he was indeed Christ, the Son of God:

"You have said so," Jesus replied. "But I say to all of you: From now on you will see the Son of Man sitting at the right hand of the Mighty One and coming on the clouds of heaven."

(Mt 26:64)

As high priest, Caiaphas, if he was the questioner of Jesus at this time, should have spotted the references encapsulated in his prisoner's reply. Psalm 110 refers to a mysterious 'lord' who will sit on the right-hand side of God, crush his enemies and heap up piles of dead bodies. This ruler will be a priest forever: Jewish interpreters sometimes see this figure as a promised king, whereas Christians have tended to interpret this psalm as a prophecy of the coming of Jesus.

Likewise, at Daniel 7:13 we are told about a human being or 'son of man' who, Daniel prophesies in a dream, will come 'with the clouds of heaven':

He was given authority, glory and sovereign power; all nations and peoples of every language worshipped him. His dominion is an everlasting dominion that will not pass away, and his kingdom is one that will never be destroyed.

Whether he recognised the references or not, the high priest's reaction was to declare that Jesus had blasphemed. He tore his clothes – an ancient Jewish sign of grief – and asked for a sentence from the assembly. 'He deserves death' they answered; and members of the crowd punched, slapped and spat on the prisoner.

Whether Jesus was interviewed by Annas then Caiaphas that night, or by both together, or by Caiaphas alone, and in what place or places this interview or these interviews took place, it is clear from Matthew that 'all the chief priests and the elders of the people' met again the next morning to decide exactly how the death of Jesus could be accomplished. They decided to bind him and take him across town to Pontius Pilate.

By far the most detailed account of Jesus' encounter with Pilate is to be found in the gospel of John, but although the details are fascinating, illuminating and very dramatic, it is unclear whether they reflect what actually happened, or are merely later embellishments. Of the synoptic gospels, Luke is the most informative in this area, but none of the gospels are explicit about Caiaphas himself being anywhere nearby when Jesus was with Pilate. In Luke, and only in Luke, Pilate learns that Jesus is from Galilee and sends him to Herod Antipas, tetrarch of Galilee, who is conveniently nearby in Jerusalem, having come up for the Passover festival. Like Pilate, Antipas can see no reason to condemn Jesus to death, and sends him back to Pilate. This means that, as in Jesus' encounter with the Jewish authorities early that morning and the previous night, there are two distinct parts to his impromptu 'trial' before Pilate.

When Jesus is before both Pilate and Herod Antipas in Luke, a group that we at first assume to be the same as the chief priests, elders and scribes who consulted about Jesus early in the morning are standing nearby, accusing Jesus of various crimes, describing him as a threat, demanding his crucifixion and insisting that Barabbas, described in Luke as a violent insurrectionist, should be released instead of Jesus.

When Jesus is before Pilate, it seems that there is also a crowd of ordinary people there, whose feelings about the Galilean are identical to those of the chief priests, elders and scribes. Whether these people followed Jesus, and his guards, captors and accusers to Pilate's praetorium, whether they materialised as if by magic as news spread that a public trial was afoot, or whether they were summoned in some way by the Jewish authorities is unclear.

The source of the accusations against Jesus is certainly the group including the chief priests, elders and scribes, and in Luke's account these accusations seem to have been tweaked so as to make the Galilean seem particularly threatening to the Roman authorities as represented by Pilate.

If, as seems likely, the high priest who interviewed Jesus appreciated all of the implications in the Galilean's utterance about coming in the clouds and sitting at the right hand of God, then, whether or not he was Caiaphas himself, he would have understood that Jesus was claiming to be the mysterious 'son of man' mentioned by Daniel. By the time Jesus and his accusers arrive at Pilate's praetorium, the Jewish authorities are accusing him of being something rather different – an itinerant agitator against Rome, a perverter of the Jewish nation and a claimant to the titles of Messiah and King of the Jews. At Luke 23:5 Jesus' accusers are careful to point out that the prisoner started stirring up the people in Galilee. As we have seen, the zealots were particularly associated with this region, but instead of panicking Pilate into sentencing Jesus to immediate death on the suspicion that he is just another dangerous Galilean zealot, Pilate uses his new knowledge of Jesus' status as a Galilean as an excuse to send him to Herod Antipas.

When Antipas can still find no reason to condemn Jesus, and sends him back to the Roman prefect, Pilate reluctantly resumes his trial of the Galilean. In the face of insistence from the assembled Jews that he should do away with the prisoner, he offers to 'chastise' him, meaning subject him to some form of corporal punishment, as a compromise, but still the assembly calls for Jesus' crucifixion, and Pilate at last consents.

6. Caiaphas after Jesus

Whether Caiaphas was personally present at both stages of Jesus' trial before the Jewish authorities, or when the Galilean was being tried before Pilate, or even when he encountered Herod Antipas, the last time his name appears in the New Testament is in the fourth chapter of the Acts of the Apostles.

Here, as often happens when Caiaphas appears in the New Testament, his name is coupled with that of Annas. Both the high priest and his father-in-law are present with 'the rulers, the elders and the teachers of the law' and 'others of the high priest's family' at a sort of hearing, where they question St Peter and a number of his followers (Acts 4:5-6). These people had been confronted and arrested in the Temple on the previous evening by 'the priests and the captain of the temple guard and the Sadducees' because they were teaching about Jesus, whose story naturally tended to reinforce the idea of the resurrection of the dead, which the Sadducees in particular denied.

Earlier that day, Peter and his followers had attracted attention when Peter had healed a lame beggar who sat every day at the aforementioned Beautiful Gate of the Temple. After their night in prison, Caiaphas, Annas and the others questioned Peter and John about their activities. In response, Peter declared that the healing of the man, who is standing there with them, was done in the name of Jesus

Christ. Peter's answers astonish those present because they come from such an apparently ordinary, unlettered man. The questioners then ask Peter and John to stop spreading the word about Jesus; which the saints say they are unable to do. Since they have committed no crime, and the healed man is there for everyone to see, the authorities are forced to let them go.

Like many of the short accounts of fascinating incidents to be found in the New Testament, this story raises more questions than it answers. Were the group who arrested Peter and his followers on the previous day sent by Caiaphas, or was Caiaphas among them? Did Caiaphas himself question Peter and John directly? Did he, as high priest, dominate the next morning's proceedings in some way? Had he been monitoring the activities of Jesus' disciples before Peter's spectacular cure at the Beautiful Gate? Is Acts correct in saying that they now had thousands of followers, and did these numbers alarm Caiaphas? Did Peter's insistence on the truth of resurrection and the afterlife offend Caiaphas as a Sadducee?

Beyond the New Testament, archaeology and the works of near-contemporary chroniclers like Josephus, there are few reliable sources on the life of Caiaphas and, as we have seen, even these sources can be unclear and contradictory. The natural Christian bias of the canonical gospels and Acts means that the opponents of Jesus, his followers and his message are often shown as deluded, weak, arbitrary and vindictive: Caiaphas is certainly in that category.

Josephus tells us that Caiaphas was deposed as high priest in 36 CE by Lucius Vitellius, the governor of Syria. In the same year, Vitellius also deposed Pontius Pilate and ordered him to return to Rome. Pilate is supposed to have been deposed as prefect of Judea because of a massacre of Samaritans that he had ordered, but it is unclear why Caiaphas had to go. A son-in-law of Annas, he was replaced by Jonathan, a son of Annas, five of whose sons eventually became high priests.

Josephus tells us about Caiaphas's sacking near the end of a long account of things Vitellius did around this time that both pleased, and showed favour to, the Jews. Chief among these was the return of some sacred priestly vestments to the Jews themselves – for years, these had been held as a kind of hostage and guarantee of good behaviour by successive Roman governors of Judea. Vitellius also abolished an unpopular tax, so it may be that his firing of Caiaphas was calculated to be a popular measure, perhaps because Caiaphas was unpopular for some reason.

It is also possible that nobody had any particular problem with Caiaphas, but that his father-in-law Annas continued to be so powerful that when he wanted to see his son, instead of his son-in-law, as high priest, he was able to make this happen. It is impossible to know how old Caiaphas was at this time, even though we know from his ossuary that he may have been sixty at the time of his death, because we do not know when he was born or when he died.

Outside of the more reliable sources, there are stories about Caiaphas in the pages of early Christian writings that have not acquired the high status of those included in the New Testament. These range from gospels and epistles that have become well-known in modern times (and which some readers feel are comparable to the canonical writings) to texts that seem merely fanciful. Some of these texts reflect the ideas of the Gnostics, who were condemned as heretics by more conventional Christians. Because some of the texts in question are drawn from Christian communities outside of Europe and the Holy Land, some of the non-canonical early Christian literature is useful in helping readers understand the diversity of Christian ideas that existed in the first centuries after Christ.

Some of the more fanciful, even whimsical non-canonical early Christian texts read like the products of wishful thinking, curiosity and speculation. Mysteries that have troubled Bible readers for centuries are laid bare in some of these writings. How did Caiaphas die? What did Jesus look like? Did he leave any writings of his own? Did the emperor Tiberius hear about Jesus? What did he think about him?

A text that frankly invents some episodes where Caiaphas interacts with the early Christians in Jerusalem, after Jesus is out of the picture, is the so-called *Clementine Recognitions*, which may date from the fourth century. This text maintains that Peter and the others felt obliged to participate in lengthy debates in Jerusalem, in which they defended their own doctrines against the arguments of various types of Jews who were resisting the new gospel, and also against Pagans.

According to 'Pseudo-Clementine', as the supposed author of the *Recognitions* is known, Caiaphas waded into one of these debates with a specific objection to one aspect of the preaching of Jesus. Jesus, he implied, taught that his followers would be rewarded for their loyalty in this life, because all their worldly needs would be met. Pseudo-Clementine may have been thinking of this passage in Matthew:

'Therefore I tell you, do not worry about your life, what you will eat or drink; or about your body, what you will wear. Is not life more than food, and the body more than clothes? Look at the birds of the air; they do not sow or reap or store away in barns, and yet your heavenly Father feeds them. Are you not much more valuable than they?

(Mt 6:25-6)

Caiaphas objects to this idea on the grounds that it cannot be found in the writings of Moses and the other authorities in what we call the Old Testament. The Christian debaters mentioned by Pseudo-Clementine have no problem in proving Caiaphas wrong on this count.

If Caiaphas and the opponents of Jesus' new message who were present at these supposed debates were not convinced by the arguments of Paul and the others, then surely they would at least have been given some pause by the extraordinary events recounted in parts of the Gospel of Nicodemus, a compilation of tales relating to this period that was probably also put together in the fourth century.

Here we learn that, after the ascension of Jesus, Joseph of Arimathea told Annas and Caiaphas that Jesus had caused many virtuous dead men to rise from their graves. Joseph was even prepared to take the high priest and his father-in-law to see them: many had assembled in his own home-town of Arimathea. The Gospel of Nicodemus exists in a number of different versions: in the version known as 'Latin B' Annas and Caiaphas do not journey to Arimathea to meet the resurrected men – the Temple hierarchy send out some trustworthy representatives, who eventually encounter 'coming down from Mount Amalech a very great multitude, about twelve thousand men, which had risen with the Lord' (trans. M.R. James).

Two of these resurrected men are prevailed upon to come to the Temple and write down their experiences. The story they set out is that of the harrowing of hell – a Christian legend that does not appear in the canonical gospels, in which Jesus storms hell like a Roman general, throws the dark kingdom into confusion and rescues many virtuous souls.

Since the two resurrected men independently write down exactly the same details, though they are carefully kept apart while they are writing, one would expect that Caiaphas and the others would be convinced that the ideas concerning the persistence of the soul of their probable sect, the Sadducees, would be rejected by them, and that they might even become Christians on the spot.

A text that is thought to date from a period some two hundred years later than the Gospel of Nicodemus implies that Caiaphas not only became a Christian, but even set about compiling records of the man he had helped to crucify. The Arabic or Syriac Infancy Gospel comprises stories about Jesus as a boy, and is supposed to be derived from the writings of Joseph Caiaphas himself.

Another Syriac document, the *Memoirs of Edessa*, tells us that though many of the Temple priests were secretly devoted to Jesus within a short time of his ascension, they did not declare this openly because they feared they would lose their lucrative and respected positions in the Jewish hierarchy. Many of their sons were, however, prepared to attend early Christian gatherings, and got in trouble with their fathers because they revealed their new Christian faith. The *Memoirs of Edessa* are supposed to be connected to the early conversion to Christianity of a kingdom called Osroene, the capital of which was called Edessa (now the city of Urfa in Turkey). Among other things, the *Memoirs* attempt to answer one of those nagging questions about Jesus – did he leave any writings of his own? The *Memoirs* include a copy of a letter from King Abgar V of Edessa, known as Abgar the Black, to Jesus himself, begging him to come to Edessa, cure Abgar's own (unnamed) illness, and remain in the city, which Abgar claims is small but still 'great enough for us both'.

The reply to this gracious invitation that Jesus supposedly dictated is also preserved in the *Memoirs of Edessa*. In this text, Jesus expresses his regret at being unable to comply with King Agbar's request in person – he will, however, see to it that one of his followers will travel to Edessa to cure Abgar and 'give life' to the people. The follower of Jesus who supposedly became a medical missionary in this way was later known as St Thaddeus of Edessa.

Two more mysteries surrounding the New Testament

narratives are laid bare in the Gospel of Nicodemus, which as we have seen is also a source for the harrowing of hell and Caiaphas's encounter with some twelve thousand resurrected men. In some versions of this apocryphal gospel we learn that the Roman emperor Tiberius, who ruled at the time of Jesus' crucifixion, certainly had heard about the Galilean holy man, and was, like Abgar the king of Edessa, anxious to see him because he also had an unnamed medical problem that he wanted fixed.

The emperor sent one of his agents to Judea to seek the man, only to find that Jesus had been crucified some time earlier. In other parts of Nicodemus, we learn that Tiberius was convinced that Jesus was indeed a genuine holy man, and even tried to have him enrolled in the official Jewish pantheon or list of gods. He is so angry to hear that Jesus is dead that he has Pilate beheaded and Annas sewn up in a hide sack that suffocates him. He orders Caiaphas to come to him in Rome, but the high priest dies *en route* on the island of Crete. The people there are unable to bury him in the conventional way: the earth itself spews him back out because of his role in the death of God. They are forced to bury him on the surface, under a pile of stones.

This story is hard to reconcile with the discovery of what is thought to be Caiaphas's ossuary near Jerusalem in 1990. It also contradicts the idea, found in some sources, that Caiaphas died by his own hand.

However Caiaphas died, the medieval Italian poet Dante had quite definite ideas about where his soul ended up. In his *Inferno*, part of the epic *Divine Comedy,* which comprises an account of the poet's own journey through hell, purgatory and heaven, the high priest is found in the sixth circle of hell among those who are being eternally punished for their hypocrisy.

Most members of this grim 'college of the hypocrites' are condemned to tramp slowly round the sixth circle while wearing heavy caps and hoods that are gold on the outside but lead within. During his brief visit to this particular infernal region, Dante talks to one of the hypocrites who can converse with him in his native Italian. This is Catalano de' Malavolti, one of two knights who were supposed to act as rulers of Dante's native Florence in 1266, when the city was threatened by violent quarrels between the rival factions of the Guelphs and Ghibellines. But instead of bringing peace, Catalano and his colleague Loderingo di Liandolo showed their hypocrisy by exploiting their position to make money and enjoy themselves.

Having established that the part of hell reserved for hypocrites could house the souls of rulers who had promised much but delivered little, Dante introduces Caiaphas without actually mentioning his name. In Carey's English blank verse translation he is:

... That pierced spirit, whom intent
Thou view'st, was he who gave the Pharisees
Counsel, that it were fitting for one man
To suffer for the people.

This of course refers to Caiaphas's comment at a meeting of the Sanhedrin, which on one level was his own justification for working for the death of Jesus, but was also an unconscious prophecy of the way Jesus' sacrifice would atone for the sins of the world (John 11:49-50).

In Canto 23 of Dante's *Inferno* we learn that Caiaphas is not tramping round with the rest of the heavily-laden 'college of hypocrites' whose ponderous headgear reflects how in life they glittered on the outside but were just a burden to the people. Instead the 'pierced soul' of Caiaphas is staked out on the path the hypocrites tramp, so that they have to walk over him. Moreover, Annas and the rest of the Sanhedrin who heard Caiaphas's prophecy are crucified on the ground in the same way:

131

. . . He doth lie
Transverse; nor any passes, but him first
Behoves make feeling trial how each weighs.
In straits like this along the foss are placed
The father of his consort, and the rest
Partakers in that council, seed of ill
And sorrow to the Jews.

The last two lines of the passage quoted above are a reminder of the medieval Christian idea that the sorrows that befell the Jewish nation shortly after the crucifixion of Jesus were richly deserved by them because they had had a hand in that execution. We have already mentioned the Jews' disastrous war against the Romans that ended in 70 CE with the near-total destruction of the Jerusalem Temple and the scattering of the Jewish people. These ideas have fed into anti-Semitism for centuries, and well within living memory Jews in supposedly enlightened countries like Britain and the United States have faced the accusation that the were the Christ-killers; cousins of Judas and stubborn adherents to a blind, legalistic faith.

While some early Christian writings, including those in the New Testament, contain stories about Caiaphas, some of which seem rather fanciful, others tackle the high priest as a philosophical or theological problem. St Augustine himself, in a letter to the Donatist Petilianus, uses the example of Caiaphas's unconscious prophecy at John 11:49-50 to show how the Donatist idea that a Christian priest should be perfect in all respects cannot hold water.

Augustine implies that Caiaphas made a true prophecy when he said that Jesus had to die for the whole nation. He was prophesying about the atonement – the idea that Christ had to die to wipe away the sins of the word – but because of his wickedness Caiaphas was not able to understand the full meaning of what he had said. If, Augustine implies, the persecutor of Christ is able to prophesy, then surely an imperfect Christian priest – who cannot possibly be as evil as Caiaphas – can make some worthwhile statements and convey some useful fragments of the truth to his flock. Augustine illustrates this idea with a striking image that contradicts the modern notion that 'the medium is the message':

In foretelling good, it is of no consequence whether the typical actions are good or bad. If it is written in red ink that the Ethiopians are black, or in black ink that the Gauls are white, this circumstance does not affect the information which the writing conveys.

Augustine is thus able to dispense with the contradictions inherent in the fact that Caiaphas, though he was evil, prophesied an event Christians regard as the most positive thing that has ever happened – the cleansing, renewing and healing of the world.

7. Gibson's Gospel

The way that Dante spreads the guilt for the crucifixion of Jesus from Caiaphas and the Sanhedrin to the whole Jewish people shows how, at least in the medieval mind, the doctrine of the atonement – that Jesus died for the sins of the whole world – was crippled and distorted by a feeling that the sins of the Jews were far worse, and far less susceptible to the cleansing power of the atonement, than those of other ethnic and religious groups.

A surprising amount of blame for the persecution of Jesus is thrown onto the Jews in the 2004 film *The Passion of the Christ*, directed by Mel Gibson. In the much earlier, and indeed more lavish, 'Jesus film' *The Greatest Story Ever Told,* a serious attempt is made to shift the blame away from the Jews, or at least to share it around, perhaps because *The Greatest Story* was released only twenty years after the full horror of the Nazi Holocaust had been revealed to the world.

As we have seen, this even-handedness in *The Greatest Story* is part of what causes the film to lose focus at times. Who is to blame? Is it Telly Savalas's thuggish, callous Pilate, Jose Ferrer's troubled, cynical Herod Antipas, or Martin Landau's sincere, youngish Caiaphas (Landau, himself a Jew, was only thirty-seven when the film was released). Or is David McCallum's misguided, guilt-ridden Judas to blame? George Stevens, the director of *The*

Greatest Story, even has Satan himself, played by the English actor Donald Pleasance, popping up at key moments so that he too can take some of the blame.

In the print of *The Greatest Story* committed to DVD for UK consumption, it is a long time before Martin Landau's Caiaphas even has a proper close-up; and in a key scene where he is trying to convict Jesus, the outspoken figure of Nicodemus appears among the Sanhedrin and makes it clear that Caiaphas has 'packed' the assembly by attempting to invite only Jesus' enemies. Nicodemus, played by another Jewish actor, Joseph Schildkraut, is just one of a series of sympathetic Jewish characters in Stevens' film. In *The Greatest Story*, far more time is devoted to Antipas than to Caiaphas, and Ferrer has such presence in the role that, even if he were given less screen-time, viewers would probably still come away from the film thinking that Antipas was the real enemy. And Claude Rains, in a brief early appearance as Antipas's father Herod the Great, makes it clear that though the Herodian family may be Jewish by religion, they are Idumeans, and not ethnically Jewish at all.

By contrast, in Gibson's *Passion of the Christ*, Herod Antipas, played by the Italian actor Luca De Dominicis, only appears in one brief scene, when he meets Jesus, who has just been sent to him by Pontius Pilate. In this scene, Antipas appears far too drunk, stupid and frivolous to be counted as a powerful enemy of Jesus.

It is hard to attach much blame to Judas in Gibson's film either, because he hangs himself fairly early on in the action. The treatment of Pilate, played by the Hungarian actor Hristo Shopov, is also remarkably sympathetic here, so that he hardly seems like a villain at all. He has tender scenes with his troubled wife Claudia (played by a real Roman Claudia, the Italian actress Claudia Gerini, born in Rome itself) and he goes to great lengths to avoid crucifying Jesus. At one point, he even confides to Claudia that he is frightened that Caiaphas may launch a rebellion against

Roman rule if he, Pilate, does not have Jesus executed.

And so, in Gibson's film, most of the blame for the execution of Jesus falls on Caiaphas, and since the Italian actor Mattia Sbragia, who plays the high priest, is usually seen in the company of other high-status Jews, Gibson's concentration on this character has been read as anti-Semitic. He is not just blaming Caiaphas – here the high priest is just one grey-bearded face in a crowd of hostile Temple priests, a crowd which also includes Annas (played by another Italian, Toni Bertorelli).

It is easy for viewers to attach a lot of blame to Caiaphas in this film because he is, unusually, present at nearly every stage of the Passion of Jesus, which is the central subject of the film. Caiaphas is even present in what is presumably supposed to be Antipas's palace in Jerusalem when Jesus encounters the tetrarch of Galilee. Here he stands with his usual escort of bearded priests in black and gold outfits.

Very near the start of *The Passion of the Christ*, Sbragia as Caiaphas is there when the thirty pieces of silver are given to (or rather thrown at) Judas, and he is prominent throughout the rowdy trial of Jesus before the Sanhedrin. During this lengthy scene, the predominant colours are black and sepia, which gives everything a suffocating, soiled look, like a dark, candle-lit room reflected in a tobacco-stained mirror. This contrasts with the cool blue colour that is predominant in Gibson's recreation of the Garden of Gethsemane.

In Gibson's version of Jesus' trial before the Sanhedrin, two Temple priests object to the proceedings against Jesus, but they are quickly shouted down and bundled out.

Sbragia's Caiaphas is also prominent in the front row of the crowd that bays for Jesus' blood before Pilate: indeed, the only way that the Roman governor can have a private word with the Galilean, away from Caiaphas's prying eyes, is by taking him behind the scenes at the praetorium. There the governor and Jesus converse in Latin.

Outside, Sbragia/Caiaphas uses humour to undermine Pilate when he addresses the crowd, and stirs them up like a born rabble-rouser, leading them in their chants - 'Crucify him!' and 'Barabbas!' Caiaphas also plays on Pilate's greatest fear – that Jesus may cause the collapse of Roman rule in Judea, or at least interrupt the flow of tax revenues. He also suggests that Jesus is trying to make himself a new King of the Jews, and claims that he, Caiaphas, and his fellow Jews in Judea have no king but Caesar. All this can just about be justified with reference to the gospels, but the gospels are less sure than Gibson about Caiaphas's role at this time. By contrast, in the equivalent scenes in George Stevens' film *The Greatest Story Ever Told*, there are always Jews in the crowd, unconnected to the Jesus group, who cry out against the harsh treatment of the Galilean.

Sbragia's Caiaphas, with his attendant priests, is also present during the prolonged, horrific scene where Gibson's Jesus, played by the American actor Jim Caviezel, is scourged by Roman soldiers on the orders of Pontius Pilate. With this scene, where Gibson's Jesus, who has already been severely beaten before the Sanhedrin, is reduced to a bloody mass, the film itself tips over into an adult-only feature, in terms of film censorship. Even here, Pilate is spared much of the blame. Unlike Caiaphas, he is not present at the scourging, and when this unbearable scene at last concludes, it is clear that the unruly Roman soldiers, who mock and man-handle their immediate superior, have gone far beyond their original orders.

Later we see Sbragia's Caiaphas at the crucifixion itself, where he speaks to Jesus as he hangs on the cross, challenging and mocking him. When it is clear that his work is done, the high priest rides off on a fine horse. Throughout, this Caiaphas shows some signs of shock and regret at the treatment of Jesus, but he does not speak up against any aspect of it, and seems determined to see it through to the very bitter end.

Even in the scene in Antipas's palace, it is clear that Caiaphas is in some sense in charge: a powerful figure who could indeed put a stop to all this, with just a word. Although Toni Bertorelli's Annas is usually present, we get no impression that he is in charge, although history and some aspects of the gospel treatment of Annas suggest that, high priest or not, he was the ultimate authority.

Although there is little in the gospels to suggest that Caiaphas was really present during so many phases of the Passion, some justification for Gibson's handling of this character can be found in documents relating to the nineteenth-century German mystic Anne Catherine Emmerich. Emmerich, a chronic invalid who spent much of her life in bed, had powerful visions that she related to the German poet Clemens Brentano. Brentano wrote these down and published them: many include insights into details of Christ's passion which Emmerich received during ecstatic visions.

As Pamela Grace points out in her book *The Religious Film* (2009) many of Emmerich's visions were distinctly anti-Semitic: she even conversed with the spirit of a long-dead Jewish woman who explained to her how the Jews used to kill Christians, including babies and children, so as to use their blood in grisly rituals. This is a version of the notorious Blood Libel, a medieval example of fake news, widely believed in the Middle Ages, which was frequently used as a justification for the persecution of the Jews. The supposed victims of these killings were sometimes turned into saints. Little St Hugh of Lincoln, a child who was found dead in that English city in 1255, was said to have been crucified by the local Jews.

It is thought that the visions of Anne Catherine Emmerich, in which, among other things, she imagined herself to be present during key scenes of the Passion, may have been induced by hallucinogenic plants she took as pain-killers. There is also a strong suggestion that Brentano, who published her visions, added a lot of his own ideas to Emmerich's.

There is little justification for Gibson's treatment of Caiaphas and the Jews in general in the gospels, and putting Emmerich's visions to the side for a moment, there are ideas to be found in modern Catholic writings that could have led Gibson, a Catholic himself, to take a different approach. In his book *Jesus at the Movies*, published in 1997, some years before the release of Gibson's *Passion*, W Barnes Tatum reproduces part of *Nostra Aetate*, a 1965 document from the Second Vatican Council. This states that 'the Jews should not be spoken of as rejected or accursed' and declares that the Church 'deplores all hatreds, persecutions, displays of anti-Semitism levelled at any time or from any source against the Jews'.

Of slightly less authority than *Nostra Aetate*, but more recent and more relevant to the business of 'Jesus films', is a very well-judged statement from the U.S. National Conference of Catholic Bishops called *Criteria for the Evaluation of Dramatizations of the Passion* (1988).

The *Criteria* implies that, at least since the release of *Nostra Aetate* in 1965, negative depictions of the Jews in dramatisations of the Passion have become unacceptable, at least to the Catholic Church. The Jews in general should not be shown as unanimous in their rejection of Jesus, and Jesus himself should not be shown as a critic of everything Jewish. The Jews should not be shown as 'avaricious' or 'bloodthirsty', and it should be made clear that some Jewish leaders and ordinary Jewish people, other than the holy family and the disciples, looked on Jesus with sympathy. Jesus' Jewish identity, and that of many of his followers, should be made explicit; and the *Criteria* specifically states that Jesus' enemies should not be 'arrayed' in 'dark, sinister costuming' when 'Jesus and his friends' are shown 'in lighter tones'. 'This can be effective on the stage,' the *Criteria* continues, 'but it can also be disastrous if the effect is to isolate Jesus and the apostles from "the Jews," as if all were not part of the same people. It is important to portray Jesus and his followers clearly as Jews among Jews, both in dress and in actions such as prayer'.

A problem with some ill-judged depictions of the Passion that the authors of the *Criteria* want to avoid is the error of depicting 'the Jews' as a monolithic, stereotyped group. The *Criteria* offers detailed advice about the diversity of the Jewish community in first-century Judea, describing the distinctions between Pharisees, Sadducees, Zealots, Herodians and others. Similar differences of opinion are perhaps reflected in a section of the Babylonian Talmud which is often cited in connection with Caiaphas's father-in-law, Annas. Here, at Pesach 57a, we learn that the Jews at the time of Jesus were not all as whole-hearted in their support for the Temple high priests and their families as Gibson's film would suggest.

In this sub-section of the Talmudic tractate that deals with the Passover festival, various crimes committed by high priests, including Annas, and other dignitaries, are detailed. Beginning with a story about a farmer who is suspected of stealing from the poor, the tractate continues with a vague tale of 'powerful people' stealing wood from the poor of Jericho, and a more detailed account of 'the powerful priests' taking more than their fair share of the valuable hides of animals sacrificed in the Jerusalem Temple.

The tractate then gets more specific, identifying the high priests of the family of Boethus and those of Annas's family as guilty of beating people with clubs, and rumour-mongering, respectively. Other high-priestly families are also identified in this text as being guilty of lying, and ordering their servants to punch people. Moving on to the source of such criticism, the text identifies 'the people in the Temple courtyard' who cried out against priests who dishonoured and desecrated the Temple, including one

Yissakhar of Kfar Barkai, who insisted on touching the Temple vessels only when his fingers were covered with silk scarves. As a consequence of this, God inspired the king of this time to cut off both of the fastidious Yissakhar's hands. Another reason for Yissakhar's mutilation was his ignorance – before the king, he had demonstrated his inability to comment in an informed way during a dispute about different types of animal sacrifices.

Bearing in mind that the Babylonian Talmud was compiled centuries after the destruction of the Jerusalem Temple, one might have expected the compilers to be looking back with longing and nostalgia when they tackled that place and its personnel, but tractate Pesach 57a shows that memories of the low standards of some of the high-priestly families in particular still survived, and it was felt that they needed to be preserved.

The tractate states that, in the case of the hides of the sacrificed animals, the powerful priests were able to take more than their fair share 'by virtue of their lineage'. The text also gives an attractive example of what could happen if the power of these well-born men was resisted. We are told that those who had bought the sacrificial animals in the first place consecrated them in such a way that all the money from their sale would be ploughed directly back into the Temple: it could no longer line the pockets of members of the priestly aristocracy. With the resulting income, it was possible to cover the whole of the inside of the sanctuary with thick plates of gold.

It is possible that the various crimes attributed to several priestly dynasties in Pesach 57a could be switched around, so that, for instance, Annas's family could be accused of physical violence and direct lying as well as just spreading ugly rumours. The problem is that, however it is understood, the passage cannot easily be applied directly to Caiaphas, who only married into this troubled dynasty, or even to Annas. Once again, as in the case of Caiaphas's last New

Testament appearance, in the book of Acts, Caiaphas's character, and what he did and said, seem to slip away from us.

In Mattia Sbragia's last scene as Caiaphas in Mel Gibson's film *The Passion of the Christ*, the stiff-necked high priest seems finally to understand the tragic nature of the events he has brought about. As Jesus dies on the cross, an earthquake shakes the Temple, and the veil that hides the Holy of Holies is torn away. Caiaphas burns his hand on a lamp that the earthquake has tipped over – an inkling, perhaps, of the eternity he might be consigned to in hell's lake of fire.

The eternal fate Dante allots to Caiaphas, staked out forever on a dismal path, endlessly trampled by ponderous hypocrites, has no element of fire in it, and it is up to individual readers of the *Inferno* to decide whether Dante has judged Caiaphas fairly, whether he really ended up in hell at all, or whether Caiaphas the probable Sadducee was right in believing that there was no hell nor any kind of afterlife lying in wait for the dead.

We do now know with a reasonable degree of certainty where Caiaphas's bones ended up, and even that he died at around the age of sixty. The characteristics of his ossuary and the family tomb in which it was placed seem to offer the chance to arrive at an overall picture of Caiaphas and his role both in history and in the central drama of the Christian story.

This picture would show Caiaphas as a man from a fairly modest priestly family who found himself occupying the high priesthood of the Jerusalem temple because his father-in-law Annas had been deposed from that position by the Romans, and because as a son-in-law of that very influential man he could be shoe-horned into the position without too much loss of face for Annas's own distinguished dynasty. It would seem, from the way that the gospel writers frequently place Annas with Caiaphas at the centre of the

Passion narrative, that Annas continued to be influential: so much so, in fact, that more than forty years after the events they recount, the writers of the gospels were not entirely sure whether Annas wasn't still high priest at the time. Something about Caiaphas's approach to the high priestly office made it possible for him to continue in the job for some eighteen years, although the Romans probably felt that they had the right to depose him at any time. Eventually, however, Caiaphas was deposed.

If it had not been for his involvement in the impromptu trial of a certain Galilean, the name of Caiaphas might be as obscure to Christian readers as the names of his successors as high priest: Jonathan, Theophilus and Matthias, all of whom were sons of Annas.

The extent to which Caiaphas really was involved in the trial or trials of Jesus is unclear. When was he present and when was he absent? When he was present, when was Annas with him, and to what extent was Caiaphas in charge? Who was it who really motivated the start of the plot to capture Jesus: the plot that may already have been on foot when a man called Judas made it known that, for a price, there was certain information he might be willing to disclose?

EXTRACTS FROM JOSEPHUS'S *JEWISH WAR* (trans. Whiston)

1. THE INNER PART OF THE TEMPLE

As to the holy house itself, which was placed in the midst [of the inmost court], that most sacred part of the temple, it was ascended to by twelve steps; and in front its height and its breadth were equal, and each a hundred cubits, though it was behind forty cubits narrower; for on its front it had what may be styled shoulders on each side, that passed twenty cubits further. Its first gate was seventy cubits high, and twenty-five cubits broad; but this gate had no doors; for it represented the universal visibility of heaven, and that it cannot be excluded from any place. Its front was covered with gold all over, and through it the first part of the house, that was more inward, did all of it appear; which, as it was very large, so did all the parts about the more inward gate appear to shine to those that saw them; but then, as the entire house was divided into two parts within, it was only the first part of it that was open to our view. Its height extended all along to ninety cubits in height, and its length was fifty cubits, and its breadth twenty. But that gate which was at this end of the first part of the house was, as we have already observed, all over covered with gold, as was its whole wall about it; it had also golden vines above it, from which clusters of grapes hung as tall as a man's height. But then this house, as it was divided into two parts, the inner part was lower than the appearance of the outer, and had golden doors of fifty-five cubits altitude, and sixteen in breadth; but before these doors there was a veil of equal largeness with the doors. It was a Babylonian curtain, embroidered with blue, and fine linen, and scarlet, and purple, and of a contexture that was truly wonderful. Nor was this mixture of colours without its mystical interpretation, but was a kind of image of the universe; for by the scarlet there seemed to be enigmatically signified fire, by the fine flax the earth, by the blue the air, and by the purple the sea; two of them having their colors the foundation of this resemblance; but the fine flax and the purple have their own origin for that foundation, the earth producing the one, and the sea the other. This curtain had also embroidered upon it all that was mystical in the heavens, excepting that of the [twelve] signs, representing living creatures.

2. THE SACRED GARMENTS OF THE HIGH PRIEST

When he officiated, he had on a pair of breeches that reached beneath his privy parts to his thighs, and had on an inner garment of linen, together with a blue garment, round, without seam, with fringe work, and reaching to the feet. There were also golden bells that hung upon the fringes, and pomegranates intermixed among them. The bells signified thunder, and the pomegranates lightning. But that girdle that tied the garment to the breast was embroidered with five rows of various colors, of gold, and purple, and scarlet, as also of fine linen and blue, with which colors we told you before the veils of the temple were embroidered also. The like embroidery was upon the ephod; but the quantity of gold therein was greater. Its figure was that of a stomacher for the breast. There were upon it two golden buttons like small shields, which buttoned the ephod to the garment; in these buttons were enclosed two very large and very excellent sardonyxes, having the names of the tribes of that nation engraved upon them: on the other part there hung twelve stones, three in a row one way, and four in the other; a sardius, a topaz, and an emerald; a carbuncle, a jasper, and a sapphire; an agate, an amethyst, and a ligure; an onyx, a beryl, and a chrysolite;

upon every one of which was again engraved one of the forementioned names of the tribes. A mitre also of fine linen encompassed his head, which was tied by a blue ribbon, about which there was another golden crown, in which was engraven the sacred name [of God]: it consists of four vowels. However, the high priest did not wear these garments at other times, but a more plain habit; he only did it when he went into the most sacred part of the temple, which he did but once in a year, on that day when our custom is for all of us to keep a fast to God.

EXTRACTS FROM JOSEPHUS'S *ANTIQUITIES OF THE JEWS* (trans. Whiston)

CHAPTER 10. An Enumeration Of The High Priests.

1. And now I think it proper and agreeable to this history to give an account of our high priests; how they began, who those are which are capable of that dignity, and how many of them there had been at the end of the war. In the first place, therefore, history informs us that Aaron, the brother of Moses, officiated to God as a high priest, and that, after his death, his sons succeeded him immediately; and that this dignity hath been continued down from them all to their posterity. Whence it is a custom of our country, that no one should take the high priesthood of God but he who is of the blood of Aaron, while every one that is of another stock, though he were a king, can never obtain that high priesthood. Accordingly, the number of all the high priests from Aaron, of whom we have spoken already, as of the first of them, until Phanas, who was made high priest during the war by the seditious, was eighty-three; of whom thirteen officiated as high priests in the wilderness, from the days of Moses, while the tabernacle was standing, until the people came into Judea, when king Solomon erected the temple to God; for at the first they held the high priesthood till the end of their life, although afterward they had successors while

they were alive. Now these thirteen, who were the descendants of two of the sons of Aaron, received this dignity by succession, one after another; for their form of government was an aristocracy, and after that a monarchy, and in the third place the government was regal. Now the number of years during the rule of these thirteen, from the day when our fathers departed out of Egypt, under Moses their leader, until the building of that temple which king Solomon erected at Jerusalem, were six hundred and twelve. After those thirteen high priests, eighteen took the high priesthood at Jerusalem, one in succession to another, from the days of king Solomon, until Nebuchadnezzar, king of Babylon, made an expedition against that city, and burnt the temple, and removed our nation into Babylon, and then took Josadek, the high priest, captive; the times of these high priests were four hundred and sixty-six years, six months, and ten days, while the Jews were still under the regal government. But after the term of seventy years' captivity under the Babylonians, Cyrus, king of Persia, sent the Jews from Babylon to their own land again, and gave them leave to rebuild their temple; at which time Jesus, the son of Josadek, took the high priesthood over the captives when they were returned home. Now he and his posterity, who were in all fifteen, until king Antiochus Eupator, were under a democratical government for four hundred and fourteen years; and then the forementioned Antiochus, and Lysias the general of his army, deprived Onias, who was also called Menelaus, of the high priesthood, and slew him at Berea; and driving away the son [of Onias the third], put Jaeimus into the place of the high priest, one that was indeed of the stock of Aaron, but not of that family of Onias. On which account Onias, who was the nephew of Onias that was dead, and bore the same name with his father, came into Egypt, and got into the friendship of Ptolemy Philometor, and Cleopatra his wife, and persuaded them to make him the high priest of that temple which he built to God in the prefecture of Heliopolis, and this in imitation of that at

Jerusalem; but as for that temple which was built in Egypt, we have spoken of it frequently already. Now when Jacimus had retained the priesthood three years, he died, and there was no one that succeeded him, but the city continued seven years without a high priest. But then the posterity of the sons of Asamoneus, who had the government of the nation conferred upon them, when they had beaten the Macedonians in war, appointed Jonathan to be their high priest, who ruled over them seven years. And when he had been slain by the treacherous contrivance of Trypho, as we have related some where, Simon his brother took the high priesthood; and when he was destroyed at a feast by the treachery of his son-in-law, his own son, whose name was Hyrcanus, succeeded him, after he had held the high priesthood one year longer than his brother. This Hyrcanus enjoyed that dignity thirty years, and died an old man, leaving the succession to Judas, who was also called Aristobulus, whose brother Alexander was his heir; which Judas died of a sore distemper, after he had kept the priesthood, together with the royal authority; for this Judas was the first that put on his head a diadem for one year. And when Alexander had been both king and high priest twenty-seven years, he departed this life, and permitted his wife Alexandra to appoint him that should be high priest; so she gave the high priesthood to Hyrcanus, but retained the kingdom herself nine years, and then departed this life. The like duration [and no longer] did her son Hyrcanus enjoy the high priesthood; for after her death his brother Aristobulus fought against him, and beat him, and deprived him of his principality; and he did himself both reign, and perform the office of high priest to God. But when he had reigned three years, and as many months, Pompey came upon him, and not only took the city of Jerusalem by force, but put him and his children in bonds, and sent them to Rome. He also restored the high priesthood to Hyrcanus, and made him governor of the nation, but forbade him to wear a diadem. This Hyrcanus ruled, besides his first nine years, twenty-four years more, when Barzapharnes and Pacorus, the generals of the Parthians, passed over Euphrates, and fought with Hyrcanus, and took him alive, and made Antigonus, the son of Aristobulus, king; and when he had reigned three years and three months, Sosius and Herod besieged him, and took him, when Antony had him brought to Antioch, and slain there. Herod was then made king by the Romans, but did no longer appoint high priests out of the family of Asamoneus; but made certain men to be so that were of no eminent families, but barely of those that were priests, excepting that he gave that dignity to Aristobulus; for when he had made this Aristobulus, the grandson of that Hyrcanus who was then taken by the Parthians, and had taken his sister Mariarmne to wife, he thereby aimed to win the good-will of the people, who had a kind remembrance of Hyrcanus [his grandfather]. Yet did he afterward, out of his fear lest they should all bend their inclinations to Aristobulus, put him to death, and that by contriving how to have him suffocated as he was swimming at Jericho, as we have already related that matter; but after this man he never intrusted the priesthood to the posterity of the sons of Asamoneus. Archelaus also, Herod's son, did like his father in the appointment of the high priests, as did the Romans also, who took the government over the Jews into their hands afterward. Accordingly, the number of the high priests, from the days of Herod until the day when Titus took the temple and the City, and burnt them, were in all twenty-eight; the time also that belonged to them was a hundred and seven years. Some of these were the political governors of the people under the reign of Herod, and under the reign of Archelaus his son, although, after their death, the government became an aristocracy, and the high priests were intrusted with a dominion over the nation. And thus much may suffice to be said concerning our high priests.

Select Bibliography

Barnes Tatum, W: *Jesus at the Movies*, Polebridge, 1997

Bernheim, Pierre-Antoine, *James, Brother of Jesus*, SCM, 1997

Bond, Helen K.: *Caiaphas: Friend of Rome and Judge of Jesus?*, Westminster John Knox, 2004

Brandon, S.G.F.: *The Trial of Jesus of Nazareth*, Batsford, 1968

Edersheim, Alfred: *The Temple: Its Ministry and Services*, Nabu, 2010

Eppstein, Victor: *The Historicity of the Gospel Account of the Cleansing of the Temple*, Zeitschrift für die neutestamentliche Wissenschaft, Volume 55, Issue 1, 1964

Evans, Craig A.: *Jesus and His World*, SPCK, 2012

Evans, Craig A.: *Jesus and the Remains of His Day*, Hendrickson, 2015

Grace, Pamela: *The Religious Film*, Wiley-Blackwell, 2009

Grant, Robert M.: *A Historical Introduction to the New Testament*, Collins, 1963

Green, Joel B.: *The Gospel of Luke*, Eerdmans, 1997

James, M.R. (trans.): *The Apocryphal New Testament*, Oxford, 1953

Josephus: *Jewish Antiquities*, Wordsworth, 2006

Josephus: *The Jewish War*, Penguin, 1959

Marshall, Alfred (ed.): *The Interlinear Greek-English New Testament*, Samuel Bagster, 1959

Pfeiffer, Robert H: *History of New Testament Times*, Adam and Charles Black, 1949

Philo Judaeus (trans. Charles Yonge): *Works*, Bohn, 1854-5

Plutarch: *The Fall of the Roman Republic*, Penguin, 1972

Rieu, E.V. (trans.): *The Four Gospels*, Penguin, 1952

Ritmeyer, Leen and Kathleen: *Jerusalem in the Year 30 AD*, Carta, 2015

Smallwood, E. Mary: *The Jews Under Roman Rule*, Brill, 2001

Suetonius: *The Twelve Caesars*, Penguin, 2003

Tacitus: *Annals*, Oxford, 2008

Webb, Simon: *What Do We Know About Pontius Pilate?* Langley Press, 2018

What Do We Know About
Herod Antipas?

1. Under the Moon

It has been said that Oscar Wilde's play *Salome* is most appreciated wherever the English language is *not* spoken. First written in French by Wilde in 1891, rehearsals in London were halted in 1892 because of a long-standing ban on the depiction of biblical characters on the English capital's stages.

Given the immense efforts being made by some Victorians to bring their contemporaries to Christ, it may seem odd that the Lord Chamberlain, who was ultimately responsible for theatre censorship in London until 1968, should have insisted on keeping Jesus, Moses and the rest off the stages of the West End. Wasn't it possible that some godless person who would never dream of reading the Bible or any other religious book might see a theatrical presentation of, say, the Passion of Christ, and be saved?

If anyone had challenged the Lord Chamberlain of the time with this idea, he might have been tempted to send the challenger a copy of the English version of Wilde's *Salome*, which was published in 1894 (the play could be published in the UK, but not performed in London). Even if the recipient of the Lord Chamberlain's gift did not read the play, he might have understood that the drama was somewhat decadent just by examining Aubrey Beardsley's classic illustrations, with their disturbing use of nudity and their sadomasochistic overtones.

Although it is just possible that someone might have been persuaded to live a more Christian life by reading or seeing Wilde's *Salome*, the author seems not to have had evangelical ideas in mind when he wrote it. To the starchier type of Victorian who came across this strange little playbook, *Salome* probably read like an attempt to use the New Testament story of the execution of John the Baptist to write highly-wrought prose poetry for the stage, and to explore unsettling themes such as incest, homosexuality, homo-eroticism and even necrophilia. It is hard to imagine how the following speech, delivered by Salome herself near the end of the play, would have gone over with a Victorian audience. Here the princess is addressing the severed head of 'Jokanaan', Wilde's name for John the Baptist:

Ah! I have kissed thy mouth, Jokanaan, I have kissed thy mouth. There was a bitter taste on thy lips. Was it the taste of blood? . . . But perchance it is the taste of love . . . . They say that love hath a bitter taste . . . . But what of that? what of that? I have kissed thy mouth, Jokanaan.

Too short to be part of a conventional evening at the theatre, and too strange to be a popular hit, Wilde's *Salome* also requires, for the title role, a palely beautiful young actress who can also dance, and is prepared to appear naked, or at least very scantily clad, in front of a live audience. In the twenty-first century, when we no longer tolerate Caucasian actors 'blacking up' to play people of African, Asian or Middle-Eastern ethnicity, a modern production would also require a mixed-race cast, which might be hard to assemble.

Richard Strauss's masterful 1905 opera of *Salome* has proved enduring, although here the requirement for a soprano who can also dance has meant that Salome's Dance of the Seven Veils is often performed by a dancer and not by the soprano at all. Another opera, a ballet, feature films and many paintings, as well as Gustave's Flaubert's story

Herodias, which influenced Wilde, have, if nothing else, allowed Herod Antipas, the subject of this book, to live outside of the pages of the New Testament and ancient history.

2. Herod's Dynasty

In the New Testament gospels, it is Herod Antipas, tetrarch of Galilee and Perea, who is responsible for ordering the execution of John the Baptist; though Wilde, the gospels and other sources would agree that other people, including Herod's wife Herodias and his step-daughter Salome, contributed to his decision.

At this point it is crucial to define exactly who Antipas was, apart from being the man responsible for the death of the Baptist; not least because the Bible and history have recorded a number of famous Herods, and it is important not to mix them up.

The first Herod mentioned by name in the Bible is Herod the Great, father of Antipas, whom the Gospel of Matthew tells us interrogated the Magi (the Wise Men or Kings who came to Judea from the east to find the Messiah) and massacred the infants of Bethlehem so that a new King of the Jews would not grow up to challenge him or his successors. The last Herod mentioned in the Bible is almost certainly supposed to be Herod Agrippa, King of Judea and a grandson of Herod the Great, whose sudden death is described in the Book of Acts (Acts 12:19).

All three of these biblical Herods; Herod the Great, Herod Antipas and Herod Agrippa, were leading members of the so-called Herodian dynasty, which supplied a number of kings and other rulers in what we now call the Holy Land for about two hundred years, stretching from roughly a century before to a century after the birth of Christ. The dynasty certainly spawned a lot of men called Herod – some of whom have left little mark on history. Even the addition of second names like 'Antipas', 'Antipater' or 'Agrippa' does not always help us to tell some of these Herods apart – there were several Herod Antipaters, for instance. The women of the dynasty also tended to have recycled names: the Salome of Wilde's play was by no means the only Salome, and there were several Mariamnes: Herod the Great even managed to marry two of these, and a third was sister to Antipas's wife Herodias, the mother of Wilde's Salome.

The confusion caused by the Herodians' evidently rather limited pool of acceptable names is further exacerbated in the case of Herod the Great by the fact that he had nine wives, by seven of whom he had children. The family tree of the dynasty can also seem a little tangled in places, because although there certainly were marriages to people from other families, the dynasty also went in for marriages to close relatives. Herod the Great is known to have married both a cousin and a niece, and Herodias, who was married to Herod Antipas when he ordered the death of John the Baptist, had previously been married to Antipas's elder half-brother Herod II. She was also the daughter of their half-brother Aristobulus IV.

In Wilde's play, Antipas is surrounded by the guests at his birthday dinner, and this number includes a contingent of Jews, whose attitudes as represented in the drama contrast in key ways with those of Antipas, his wife Herodias and her daughter Salome. Wilde clearly wants us to identify these members of the Herodian dynasty as something other than Jews, and also something other than the Romans who are also present, whom Salome herself finds 'brutal and coarse, with their uncouth jargon. Ah! how I loathe the Romans!' She adds; 'They are rough and common, and they give themselves the airs of noble lords.'

160

In fact the dynasty of the Herods was Jewish by religion, though they were Idumeans who originated from the area called Edom, south of the Dead Sea. The Idumeans, who were supposed to be the descendants of Esau, the hairy twin brother of Jacob in Genesis, had been conquered by the Jewish leader John Hyrcanus around 125 BCE, and forcibly converted to Judaism. But members of the dynasty gained power throughout the region not just by using their leadership skills on the local Jews – they also inspired confidence among various non-Jewish allies in the region, and were so adept at exploiting the Roman presence there for their own ends that they must sometimes have seemed more like Romans than Jews.

Herod the Great, by some distance the most influential of these Herodian rulers, was probably born in the 70s BCE, and was able to rise to prominence because of the ever-shifting nature of the local political and military situation. This Herod, Antipas's father, built on the dynasty-building work of his own father, Herod Antipater, who had made himself a prominent figure during the last years of the Jewish Hasmonean dynasty.

Herod the Great experienced real power for the first time when he was only in his twenties, when in 47 BCE he was appointed governor of Galilee, the northern region that was later to become the birthplace of Jesus Christ, and also part of the inheritance of Herod Antipas. Herod's appointment was made possible by the fact that his own father, the aforementioned Herod Antipater, was a supporter of Hyrcanus II, a Jewish high priest and also a grandson of the John Hyrcanus who had conquered the Idumeans over seventy years earlier. This second Hyrcanus had been appointed Ethnarch of Judea by Julius Caesar, also in 47 BCE, but he was always swayed by Antipater's advice; and by this time Judea was in any case a client state of Rome, and puppet rulers like Hyrcanus could not claim ultimate power any more.

The man who later became known as Herod the Great might have spent the rest of his life happily ruling Galilee, while his older brother Phasael reigned as governor of Jerusalem, and Hyrcanus II remained as 'Ethnarch'; but seven years after this arrangement was put in place Hyrcanus's brother Antigonus invaded with help from the Parthian Empire, based in modern Iran and Iraq. Antigonus seized control, and either had Hyrcanus's ears cut off or bit them off himself so that he could never again become High Priest of the Jews (to be admitted into the higher ranks of the priesthood, men had to be free of deformities, certain diseases and also certain types of permanent injury).

Antigonus's invasion must have seemed to many of the locals like a disaster for Herod, but in fact he was able to turn the situation to his own advantage. He travelled to Rome to seek help and was unexpectedly named King of the Jews by the Roman senate. With Roman help, Herod was able to turn this grand title into a real kingdom, and after three years of war he became King of Judea, probably in 36 BCE. He ruled as such for some thirty-seven years, until his death, which may have happened as late as 1 CE, when he was over seventy years old.

To have lived so long and died of natural causes in such bloodthirsty times, and when medicine was in such a primitive state, was an achievement in itself; but Herod the Great, the father of Herod Antipas, had other achievements to boast of.

His wealth and power allowed him to be a prodigious builder. According to the Jewish historian Josephus he restored and greatly extended the Temple complex in Jerusalem, then the focal point of world Judaism. He also built a large palace for himself in Jerusalem, and founded a city, named Sebaste in honour of the Roman emperor Augustus, in Samaria, as well as other cities that he called Caesarea. These cities tended to feature Pagan temples dedicated to Augustus and, as Josephus says, 'there was not any place of his kingdom fit for the purpose that was permitted to be without somewhat that was for Caesar's honour'.

One of Herod the Great's new cities was Caesarea Maritima, a port city of gleaming white marble on the Mediterranean coast. Here huge stones were built up to form a safe artificial harbour, many fine buildings and statues were erected, and there was a temple to Augustus with a colossal statue of the first emperor inside it. Also at Caesarea Maritima, Herod the Great built a market, an amphitheatre and a theatre, and founded Caesar's Games, which were to take place once every five years.

As well as building in honour of the Roman emperor, Herod the Great rebuilt the coastal city of Anthedon and re-named it for his friend Agrippa. He also named a new city Antipatris after his father, named a building at Jericho after his mother, and named a tower at Jerusalem for his brother Phasaelis.

Despite the apparent affection for family members that he displayed by naming buildings after them, Herod the Great's marked paranoia caused him to suspect many of his relatives of plotting against him. This led to his killing one of his wives and three of his sons, as well as the aforementioned Hyrcanus II, who was the grandfather of the first of Herod's wives to be called Mariamne, the wife he had killed.

Given the paranoia that did not allow him to spare even close family members violent deaths, it would seem consistent with Herod the Great's character that he would have ordered the Massacre of the Innocents described in the Gospel of Matthew. But Herod's alleged attempt to kill the Messiah by wiping out all boys in Bethlehem aged two and under does not appear in any of the other three New Testament gospels, and, unlike many details of Herod's career, the massacre is not mentioned in Josephus or in the works of other ancient historians.

The suspicion that led Herod the Great to murder one of his wives and three of his sons also led him to exclude another son, Herod II, from the succession, which meant that Herod Antipas was able to inherit a sizeable portion of his father's kingdom, although he was only his sixth son, born of his fourth wife, when his father Herod the Great was in his fifties. Antipas was, moreover, probably only in his twenties when he found himself a tetrarch.

When Herod the Great died, his territories were divided up, according to the will he had hastily changed just before his death, between his surviving sons by three different wives whom he did not suspect of having plotted against him. (It is important to note that in his previous will he had named his son Herod Antipas, the subject of this book, the sole heir of his wealth and power). In this will, a small area was also allotted to Herod's sister, Salome.

The arrangement was approved by the emperor Augustus: Antipas got Galilee in the north, and Perea, which stretched along much of the eastern shore of the River Jordan. These territories were separated by a stretch of land called the Decapolis that straddled the Jordan and was dominated by cities that were theoretically independent of both Rome and the Herodian dynasty. Antipas's 'moth-eaten' tetrarchy was therefore bordered at different points by territories controlled by his full brother Archelaus and his half-brother Philip respectively. From part of Perea he could look across the Jordan at the land controlled by his aunt Salome, and parts of his territories bordered Roman Syria and the lands of the Arab Nabateans to the south-east.

The lion's share of Herod the Great's territories, an area that included both Jerusalem and Caesarea, had been allotted to Antipas's older full brother, Archelaus, but this Herod, who also seems to have come into his inheritance at a very young age, soon ran into serious trouble.

Shortly before his death, Herod the Great had become embroiled in a bloody dispute with the Temple authorities in

Jerusalem. To honour his Roman masters, he had installed a magnificent golden eagle over the entrance to the inner sanctuary of the Temple, which offended many of the Jews because it went against part of the second commandment, forbidding images of animals. As a representation of an eagle, the statue also seemed inappropriately Roman to the locals; and eventually some forty young men, inspired by the inflammatory words of two rabbis, lowered themselves down on ropes to where the eagle was, and chopped it up with axes.

In response, Herod, who was now suffering pitifully under his last illness, ordered the forty young men and their rabbis to be burned alive.

The affair of the eagle might have ended with Herod's death, which quickly followed, but the Jews of Jerusalem had not forgotten the deaths of the forty young men and the rabbis, and at a public meeting with Archelaus during the festival of Passover in 4 BCE they demanded that the surviving men who had approved of their executions should be punished. Archelaus tried to put the protestors off, saying that he would make the decision when his rule had been approved by Rome; but overnight the locals were heard to be wailing loudly, mourning the deaths of the young men and their rabbis. Soon so many people were streaming into the Temple to join the protest that violence seemed imminent.

The soldiers Archelaus then sent in to calm things down only provoked violence: they were stoned, and some were killed. Archelaus then sent in a larger force, which massacred some three thousand people.

Not surprisingly, Archelaus had to face accusations of cruelty and high-handedness when he went to Rome shortly after this to ratify his position. But he was ably defended, and confirmed as ruler of Judea. He continued to be unpopular, however, and his standing with the Jewish community was not improved by the scandal of his divorce and re-marriage. He divorced one of those Mariamnes, who was the daughter of his dead half-brother Aristobulus IV, and married the widow of another of his dead half-brothers, Alexander. This lady was a princess called Glaphyra, who had to divorce her second husband Juba, King of Mauritania, to marry Archelaus.

As complex as this divorce and marriage were, with its overtones of incest, Archelaus's brother Herod Antipas almost managed to match his brother's re-marriage in complexity and potential for offence to observant Jews. Antipas married Herodias, the daughter of his dead half-brother Aristobulus IV (and therefore sister of the last Mariamne mentioned above). Herodias had to divorce her first husband, Antipas's half-brother Herod II, in order to marry Antipas, who himself had to divorce his first wife, a daughter of the King of Nabatea. This Arab king, Aretas IV, took offence at Antipas's desertion of his daughter, and, as we shall see, made a great deal of trouble for the tetrarch.

Complaints against the regime of Herod Archelaus became so serious that the emperor Augustus decided to remove him altogether. He was not, however, replaced by yet another member of the Herodian family, acting as a puppet ruler for the Romans. Augustus replaced Archelaus with a Roman prefect. If nothing else, this meant that Herod the Great's gleaming white city of Caesarea Maritima became a base for the Roman authorities. The first of the Roman prefects of Judea was Coponius, who ruled from 6 to 9 CE. Twenty years later, a man called Pontius Pilate became the fifth Roman prefect of Judea.

3. Antipas and John the Baptist

From 6 CE, Herod Antipas found himself in the personal and political position he was in when he first encountered John the Baptist some twenty-five years later. He ruled Galilee and Perea and was married to Herodias. Other parts of the region were ruled by his relations, but Judea, Idumea and Samaria were ruled directly from Rome, this ancient super-power being represented by a prefect.

It is likely that after some twenty-five years in office, Antipas, now in his forties or fifties, was used to his religious and political position as a Jew not accepted as such by many Jews; a man who had to walk a narrow path between his Pagan masters back in Rome and the Jewish religious authorities in Jerusalem, and also had to keep his head above water during the inevitable disputes between members of his tricky and sometimes murderous family.

But his job still had some surprises in store, one of them being the advent of a wild prophet of the wilderness, who wore a leather belt and clothes made of camel's hair, and lived on locusts and wild honey. This of course was John the Baptist, whose origins are described in detail in the Gospel of Luke.

John's father was an elderly Temple priest called Zechariah. He was married to Elizabeth, a relative of the girl who was later to become the mother of Jesus, who had always been unable to conceive a child. The angel Gabriel told Zechariah that Elizabeth would bear him a son, despite her great age. The son would be called John, and:

He will be a joy and delight to you, and many will rejoice because of his birth, for he will be great in the sight of the Lord. He is never to take wine or other fermented drink, and he will be filled with the Holy Spirit even before he is born. He will bring back many of the people of Israel to the Lord their God. And he will go on before the Lord, in the spirit and power of Elijah, to turn the hearts of the parents to their children and the disobedient to the wisdom of the righteous – to make ready a people prepared for the Lord.

(Lk 1:14-17)

It would seem that Herod Antipas was not one of those who rejoiced because of the birth of John the Baptist, at least not when the Word of God came to the son of Zechariah as an adult, and he began preaching repentance, and baptising in the River Jordan. According to Luke, this began in the fifteenth year of the Roman emperor Tiberius; or 29 CE.

In order to preach repentance more effectively in his sermons in the wilderness, John seems to have felt himself obliged to point out some of the reasons why his listeners needed to repent. Luke tells us that he called some of them a 'brood of vipers' (Lk 3:7) who could not claim to be children of Abraham, and who were liable to be cut down and thrown into the fire like barren fruit-trees (Lk 3:7-9). In Matthew, John reserves these comments for the Pharisees and Sadducees who come to listen to him, but he also criticises Herod Antipas directly, remarking that he had no right to take his brother's wife.

According to the Gospel of Mark, which has the longest account of the death of John the Baptist of any of the gospels, John's comments about the marriage of Antipas and

Herodias inspired the anger of Herodias in particular, and she wanted to see John dead; but Antipas would not order his execution, because he knew John to be a righteous man, and enjoyed listening to him.

But Herodias saw her chance at a birthday party of her husband's, when her daughter danced for the tetrarch. Her dance was so pleasing to Antipas and his guests, who included 'high officials and military commanders and the leading men of Galilee' (Mk 6:21) that Herod promised the girl anything she wanted as a thank-you gift, even up to half his kingdom. Having consulted with her mother, the girl asked for the head of John the Baptist on a platter. Although he was greatly distressed, Antipas felt that he had to agree, since he had made his promise in front of all his guests. He sent an executioner into the prison, who returned with the head, which the girl gave to Herodias. When they heard about his death, John's disciples came and took away his body for burial.

Although this is the fullest New Testament account of the death of the Baptist, certain details are missing that will be familiar to anyone who has read or seen Wilde's *Salome*. To begin with, neither in Mark nor in any other New Testament account do we learn the name of Herodias's daughter, who so pleased Antipas with her dance. She is traditionally identified with a daughter of Herodias known to history as Salome, but whether Antipas's dancing step-daughter really was the same girl cannot be known for sure. Another difference between Wilde's version and that to be found in the gospels is that whereas Wilde's Salome secures her step-father's promise *before* she dances, the unnamed girl in the New Testament *dances first*, and is then promised anything she desires, up to half of Antipas's kingdom.

At first the New Testament girl does not know what to ask for, and asks her mother Herodias, who tells her to ask for the Baptist's head because she, Herodias, wants to see the holy man dead. In Wilde's version, Salome herself wants

John dead because he has previously spurned her sexual advances.

In the New Testament version, Antipas seems to send for the Baptist's head fairly quickly, although he is very reluctant to do so. In Wilde's play, Antipas tries to tempt Salome with alternative gifts, including his hundred milk-white peacocks:

They will follow you whithersoever you go, and in the midst of them you will be like the moon in the midst of a great white cloud . . . . I will give them all to you. I have but a hundred, and in the whole world there is no king who has peacocks like unto my peacocks. But I will give them all to you. Only you must loose me from my oath, and must not ask of me that which you have asked of me.

Here and elsewhere in Wilde's play, it is evident that Antipas is attracted by Salome's moon-like, virginal beauty. Indeed the way he looks at his step-daughter stirs the suspicions of Herodias, the girl's mother, who at first tries to forbid Salome's dance. In the New Testament, Antipas's attraction to the girl is not made explicit.

In the play, Salome dances what Wilde calls 'The Dance of the Seven Veils', but in the Biblical account the dance is not given a specific name, and there is no description it.

At the end of Wilde's play, Antipas is so shocked by his step-daughter's behaviour that he orders her execution. The New Testament does not tell us what happened to the dancing girl, but Josephus tells us that the Salome who is often identified as the dancer lived long enough to marry twice, bear children and even become a queen by her second marriage.

Josephus also confirms the historicity of Antipas's execution of John the Baptist. In Book eighteen of his *Jewish Antiquities*, the historian, who was born less than ten years after the death of the Baptist, tells us that when Antipas suffered a terrible defeat in battle, 'some of the Jews' remembered the treatment he had meted out to John a few years earlier, and concluded that the near-total loss of his army was God's punishment. We will learn more about the reasons for, and the consequences of, this battle later.

Whereas the New Testament account, and indeed Wilde's play, throw a lot of the blame for John's death on Herodias and her daughter, these women are not mentioned in this connection by Josephus, and although John's doubts about the validity of Antipas's marriage appear in the Bible, they are not mentioned by the historian. Instead, Josephus has Antipas imprisoning and executing John, a 'good man, who had commanded the Jews to exercise virtue, righteousness towards one another and piety towards God' because he feared that, with his large numbers of obedient followers, the Baptist might be able to raise a rebellion. Antipas's execution of him is, therefore, a preventative measure, or pre-emptive strike: by killing the Baptist, Antipas thought he 'might prevent any mischief John might cause, and not bring himself into difficulties by sparing a man who might make him repent of it when it would be too late'.

Near the end of his account, Josephus tells us that 'Herod's suspicious temper' moved him to send John as a prisoner to his castle of Machaerus, a place Josephus describes in detail in his *Jewish War*. The way John's execution is described in Josephus makes it quite possible that Antipas merely sent John there to be imprisoned and then executed, without going there himself, with or without his wife or step-daughter. If Josephus's account is more accurate than those to be found in the gospels, then the whole drama of Antipas's birthday party, Salome's dance and John's severed head disappears in a puff of smoke.

Over two hundred years of archaeology at Machaerus on the east bank of the Dead Sea, in what is now Jordan, has

171

revealed a place that, in Antipas's time, could have served as the setting for the macabre spectacle described by Mark, Matthew and Oscar Wilde, if that spectacle ever took place.

Machaerus stands at the top of a steep hill which was, according to Josephus, first spotted as a useful place to put a fortress by the Jewish king Alexander Janneaus, the father of the John Hyrcanus II who was killed by Herod the Great. Under this dynasty, the Hasmoneans, which was in effect infiltrated and brought down by the Herodians, the fortress of Machaerus had been a rather Spartan outpost, built to guard the eastern approaches to Judea. It was, however, much improved by Herod the Great, who turned the inside of the main castle or citadel at the top of the rock into something like a luxurious Roman villa. In its heyday, Machaerus was supplied with water via an impressive aqueduct, but still retained cisterns for catching and storing rain-water.

On a clear day, Herod Antipas would have been able to look out from the sun-baked battlements of Machaerus and see not only Jerusalem but also the fortresses of Masada, Herodium, Hyrcania, Cypros, Doq and Alexandrium. No doubt he would have had his own thoughts about the fact that after the fall of his brother Archelaus, these strongholds were all in the hands of the Roman prefect of Judea.

The Hungarian archaeologist Győző Vörös has described a bath-house, a ground-floor *triclinium* or dining-room with arches and a storey above, a small garden, and a typically Roman courtyard with pillars, like a secular version of the cloisters of a medieval cathedral, at Machaerus. It is in this courtyard that Vörös suggests that Antipas might have witnessed Salome's dance. Wilde has this happen on a terrace opening off Antipas's dining room: a courtyard adjacent to the *triclinium* is certainly close enough. The Baptist would probably not, however, have been imprisoned in a cistern below the courtyard, as he is in Wilde's play, since the fortress's cisterns were probably still being used for their original purpose at this time. It is more likely that John would have been incarcerated in a prison in the lower part of the fortress, outside of the citadel, where a small town was enclosed by Machaerus's outer walls.

Diggers were delighted to find a semi-circular niche or apse in one wall of the courtyard at Machaerus: was this where Antipas sat enthroned to watch his step-daughter's dance?

Given that it was built and re-modelled by men who probably had little or no European blood in their veins, the look of the ruins at, and the theoretical reconstructions of, Machaerus are very Roman. The business of watching someone else dance during or after a birthday dinner was also typically Roman. The Romans themselves were not great dancers, and many aristocratic Romans thought dancing beneath their dignity. But dancers from all over the known world, alone or in troupes, would be paid to dance before the Romans as they reclined on their high dining-couches and looked on with drunken, sated and no doubt sometimes lustful eyes.

During the Great Jewish Revolt that led to the Jewish War of 66-73 CE, in which Josephus himself fought, Machaerus was used as a fortress by the Jewish Zealots who were rebelling against Roman rule. The Roman legate Lucilius Bassus set about besieging the fortress by building a rubble ramp over one of the deep ravines that surround it. The remains of this ramp have been found by modern excavators, who have also identified that it was never actually finished. Bassus brought the siege to an end before the ramp was completed by making use of a Zealot called Eleazar, whom he had managed to capture during one of the Zealots' sallies out of the castle, when their aim was to hold up the building of the ramp.

This Eleazar was stripped naked and sorely whipped in full view of the walls of Machaerus, and at the sight of this, 'the Jews were terribly confounded, and the city, with one voice, sorely lamented him, and the mourning proved greater than could well be supposed upon the calamity of a single person'. Taking advantage of the distress of the besieged Jews over the much-loved Eleazar, Bassus erected a wooden cross, so that it looked as if poor Eleazar was about to be crucified. At this, the Jews gave up the castle.

A factor that no doubt helped to tip the balance in favour of surrender was a speech of Eleazar's, delivered before the walls of Machaerus, when he asserted that the Romans had already conquered most of the known world, and were probably invincible. It is tempting to suggest that the teachings of Jesus, some forty years earlier, might have been informed by this realisation that the Romans were in the Holy Land to stay, at least for the foreseeable future. Rejecting, implicitly, the dreams of the Zealots, who believed that their land could be cleansed of the Roman contamination by military means, Jesus preached universal brotherhood, and the possibility that the Romans, and indeed all the Gentiles, had a chance to purify themselves by embracing a new covenant.

It is intriguing that the accounts of Antipas's execution of John the Baptist in Mark, Matthew and Josephus are all what we would now call 'flashbacks', in the language of modern film-makers. In Mark and Matthew, Antipas is reminded of John when he hears about Jesus travelling from place to place, preaching and performing miracles. He assumes that Jesus is John the Baptist, whom he had executed, returned from the dead. In these gospels, there then follow accounts of the fateful birthday party, the dance and the beheading.

In Josephus's *Jewish War*, it is 'some of the Jews' who remember Antipas's treatment of the Baptist, and assume that his latest disastrous military setback was a judgement sent by God. It is only when this suspicion has been established that Josephus launches into his account of John's execution.

174

In all three accounts, something in the present causes a recollection of John's life and death, so that in all three of these books the story of John's execution is not told in its correct place in the chronology.

4. Antipas, Jesus and Pontius Pilate

We have seen how in the gospels of Mark and Matthew Herod Antipas hears about Jesus' activities and immediately assumes that Jesus is none other than John the Baptist, whom he had executed, returned from the dead. When Antipas met Jesus he presumably saw that the Nazarene was somebody quite different, but the question is, did the two ever meet?

The Gospel of Luke tells us that, just before he was arrested, Jesus was confronted by a crowd including 'the chief priests, the officers of the temple guard, and the elders' (Lk 22:52) on the Mount of Olives. These newcomers were able to identify Jesus because Judas kissed him. Seeing their swords and clubs, Jesus asked why they had come armed, and at night - 'Am I leading a rebellion?' (Lk 22:52)

Jesus was then taken to the house of the High Priest, and at dawn the next morning he appeared before 'the council of the elders of the people, both the chief priests and the teachers of the law' (Lk 22:66). These men questioned him, and Jesus' answers to their questions convinced them that he believed himself to be 'The Son of God'. The whole council then rose and took Jesus to the Roman prefect, Pilate.

From Luke's account, it would seem that as they walk across Jerusalem to the *praetorium* of the Roman prefect, Jesus' accusers decide not to accuse him of claiming to be the Messiah, or Son of God, before Pilate, but to present him as a more political figure: an agitator against Roman rule: 'We have found this man subverting our nation,' they say, 'he opposes payment of taxes to Caesar and claims to be Messiah, a king.' (Lk 23:2)

Pilate asks Jesus if he is a king, and he replies, 'You have said so' (Lk 23:3). As I suggest in my book on Pontius Pilate, this may be Jesus' comment on the way that the terms 'Son of God' and 'Messiah' have been turned by his enemies into the more politically contentious title 'King of the Jews'.

Jesus' answer to his single question seems to be enough to convince Pilate that there is no crime with which he can charge Jesus. But when he explains this to 'the chief priests and the crowd' (Lk 23:4) they claim that Jesus 'stirs up the people all over Judea by his teaching. He started in Galilee and has come all the way here'. (Lk 23:5)

Hearing that Jesus started his preaching in Galilee, Pilate establishes that the prisoner is a Galilean, and sees a possible way to get Jesus' case off his hands. Since he comes from Herod's jurisdiction, he should be tried by Herod, who happens to be nearby in Jerusalem at this time of festival. So Jesus is sent off across the city again to see the tetrarch of Galilee.

Luke tells us that Antipas is delighted to see Jesus, because he has heard so much about him. He hopes he will perform a miracle for him, but he will not. He plies him with questions (none of which are recorded by Luke) but Jesus remains silent. Meanwhile, 'the chief priests and the teachers of the law' (Lk 23:10) continue to accuse the Galilean. By implication it would seem that 'the crowd' that was present at Jesus' first hearing before Pilate has not been allowed into Antipas's palace, or has not followed Jesus across the city to the tetrarch's house, if that is where this confrontation is supposed to be taking place.

Finding Jesus completely uninteresting, Antipas and his soldiers dress him up in a gorgeous robe, no doubt one of many that were kept in the palace, or travelled with the tetrarch wherever he went. Thus attired, Jesus is sent back to Pilate.

If we put Antipas's demand that Jesus should perform a miracle for him together with his attempt to mock the Galilean by dressing him up in a gorgeous robe, and his reaction to Salome's dance at Machaerus, we get the impression that the tetrarch was a voyeur, a man who liked to watch things. He enjoyed sitting back in his throne or on his Roman-style dining-couch, perhaps with wine and some snacks to hand, and turning at least some of the endless audiences and meetings he had to endure, into entertainments.

Antipas's hunger for new sights is emphasised in Pasolini's 1964 film of the Gospel of Matthew. Here Antipas is played by Francesco Leonetti, an actor with unusually large eyes and heavy, almost reptilian eye-lids. While Wilde's *Salome*, as we have seen, explores disturbing themes such as homosexuality, homo-eroticism, necrophilia and incest, Pasolini's version of Salome's dance introduces the idea that Herod Antipas is a paedophile. Paola Tedesca, the girl Pasolini chose to play Salome, was only twelve years old at the time, and her dance is extremely innocent and child-like, and she is very modestly dressed throughout. Antipas, nevertheless, looks on with lustful eyes.

Luke remarks that after Jesus is returned to Pilate dressed in his mocking, kingly robe, Pilate and Antipas, who had previously been enemies, are suddenly friends. This gives the lie to the assertion that appears later in the New Testament, in Acts 4:27, that Pilate and Herod had conspired together to plot the execution of Jesus. We are also tempted to doubt this statement in Acts when we reflect that in Luke neither Antipas nor Pilate mention any crime Jesus is supposed to have committed. Surely, if they were conspiring together to kill him, they would have cooked up some damning charge between them?

It is easy to understand why Antipas and Pilate would

not have been friends before their respective encounters with Jesus somehow reconciled them. As Roman prefect of a large area including Judea, and also including the key cities of Caesarea and Jerusalem, Pilate was in charge of many places Antipas probably thought should have been his, or at least should have remained in the hands of some member of the Herodian family. The fact that his brother Archelaus was removed from a roughly equivalent position to Pilate's might still have rankled, even after more than a decade. That Archelaus was banished by the Romans for his miss-handling of his tetrarchy might also have wounded Antipas's family pride. True, Antipas and Archelaus were sometimes enemies when both were living on their home soil, but Antipas might still have preferred his brother as a neighbouring ruler to some upstart Roman from the equestrian or knightly class. The fact that the Romans were now so powerful, in this non-European region, that they could put in a prefect in this way, must have caused widespread local resentment, even alarm.

As we have seen, Pontius Pilate was the fifth Roman prefect of Judea, which for the Romans encompassed not only Judea proper but also the Herodian homeland of Idumea, and Samaria. Pilate would eventually be called back to Rome because of his tyrannical approach, and this side of his character evidently made him unpopular with many of Antipas's fellow-countrymen. The fact that, in keeping with the policy of the emperor Tiberius, Pilate and his predecessor as prefect, Valerius Gratus, had unusually long stints in their jobs, may also have caused resentment to build up. We have already tried to imagine Antipas looking out from the battlements of his fortress at Machaerus at all the local fortresses that were now in Roman hands. In Jerusalem itself, it is likely that Pilate lived in Herod the Great's old palace when he was in the city; a fine house Antipas would at one time, before his father made out his later will, have expected to inherit on his father's death. When he himself was in Jerusalem, Antipas might have felt humiliated by the idea of having to stay in another house, when Pilate wasn't even in Herod's old palace most of the time, preferring to stay at Caesarea.

That Pilate and Antipas would have become friends after they had both questioned Jesus within a short space of time seems less likely than that they should have remained enemies, and this sudden change of heart is not explained in Luke. It is possible, however, that the fact that they both concluded that Jesus was innocent, that Antipas had agreed to see Jesus at Pilate's bidding, and that the tetrarch did not presume to punish him himself, beyond merely mocking him with a gorgeous robe, helped to heal their relationship.

On his side, Antipas might have felt gratified to be remembered by the Roman prefect as the man who ruled Galilee: the fact that Pilate knew that he was in Jerusalem at the time, presumably to celebrate the Passover festival, might also have felt like a mark of favour. He may not have been able to sit as a judge when he was in Jerusalem, under normal circumstances, since his sphere of influence was far away to the north and east. A bit of judicial business might also have made a welcome break from the social round he normally had to trudge when he was in the city.

Although Luke does not tell us this, Antipas might also have been pleased to get a close look at Jesus so that he could assure himself that he was not John the Baptist risen from the dead. As we have seen, this was a macabre suspicion that Herod entertained at one time.

The experience of sending Jesus to Antipas and then getting him back might have caused Pilate to maintain his earlier, negative view of the tetrarch, because he might have seen Jesus' return as a disappointment. Hadn't he sent the man to Herod to get rid of him? Couldn't Antipas have had him executed, or at least thrown into prison, or shipped him back to Galilee, on his own authority? Pilate may have known that Antipas had already had a similar figure, John the Baptist, executed, but this was at Machaerus, in Perea across the Dead Sea, part of Antipas's own tetrarchy.

The lizard-eyed Francesco Leonetti could not legitimately have had a scene with the actor playing Jesus in Pasolini's *Gospel of Matthew* because Antipas's role in the trial of Jesus is not related in Matthew, or indeed in Mark or John. This has led some to conjecture that Antipas was not involved at all at this point, and that Luke either invented the encounter between Herod and Jesus, or based his account of it on a faulty source.

If whoever wrote the Gospel of Luke inserted Antipas into the narrative here with no real evidence to back the insertion, then the intention of the author, or a later editor, may have been to add to the various ways Pilate tries to save Jesus from the cross. These are particularly evident in the account in John, where it is implied that the prefect might have prevaricated for as long as six hours before passing sentence on the Galilean. This is all part of the rather easy ride Pilate gets in the gospels: yes he did have Jesus crucified, but it was against his will.

Although it is tempting to doubt Antipas's participation in the trial of Jesus, it must be remembered that other crucial elements in the account of the trial or trials of Jesus in the gospels are unique to only one gospel. The intervention of Pilate's wife, who warns the prefect to have nothing to do with Jesus because she has just had a disturbing dream about him, is only mentioned in Matthew. Matthew, likewise, is our only source in the canonical gospels for Pilate's public washing of his hands to demonstrate that he will not take responsibility for the death of Jesus. If we were to reduce our understanding of the life of Jesus and the roles of people like Antipas and Pilate to what is mentioned in all four gospels, or even two or three of them, then we would be left with a decidedly moth-eaten conception of the Christian Messiah. Herod's possible role in Jesus' trial would disappear, as would, for instance, the Magi who are part of the Advent story: like Pilate's wife, these three wise men from the east only appear in Matthew.

Comparing Pilate's wife's intervention in the trial with Jesus' visit to Herod, both of which are only recorded in one gospel, it must be said that the 'wife' episode is the least likely. For one, Mrs Pilate's words seem to have no effect on the proceedings, and neither she nor her words are ever mentioned again. By contrast, in Luke Pilate refers to Herod's failure to find Jesus guilty, and tries to use this as another reason to release the Galilean (Lk 23:15).

There is nothing inherently unlikely in the idea of Pilate sending Jesus to Antipas, and it is certainly likely that the Tetrarch was in Jerusalem at this time, along with thousands of Passover pilgrims from all over the Jewish world. Outside of the canonical gospels, Antipas plays a much more central role in a fragment of a gospel that was found in the tomb of an Egyptian monk in 1886. This section from the otherwise lost Gospel of Peter has Herod Antipas present with Pontius Pilate at the trial of Jesus. Here Pilate leaves after he has washed his hands, because neither Antipas nor any of the Jews present will wash their own hands, and Antipas himself sentences Jesus to death:

But of the Jews no man washed his hands, neither did Herod nor any one of his judges: and whereas they would not wash, Pilate rose up. And then Herod the king commanded that the Lord should be taken into their hands, saying unto them: All that I commanded you to do unto him, do ye.

(trans. M.R. James)

As in the case of the Baptist's execution at Machaerus, archaeology and other forms of historical research outside of the Bible can give us an idea of what the settings for the events detailed above would have been like.

Although the Roman prefects of Judea had probably

taken over the magnificent palace of Herod the Great, the most impressive building, apart from the Temple, in the whole of Jerusalem, Antipas was probably not exactly forced to camp out when he visited the city. He most likely lived in an older house, called the Hasmonean Palace, which, like the castle of Machaerus, the Herods had inherited from the previous dynasty of rulers. Unfortunately, no trace of this building remains for archaeologists to pick over, but it is thought to have been somewhat smaller than Herod the Great's palace, and roughly equidistant between it and the Temple, with a fine view of the latter. There is no reason to suppose that this palace was not re-modelled and re-decorated under the Herods, as Machaerus had been. To judge from other fine Jerusalem houses of the period, the ruins of which have been investigated, Antipas's home-from-home in the Holy City would have had fine large rooms with frescos on the walls and intricate mosaic patterns on the floors. There would no doubt have been superb white marble paving-stones where there were no floor-mosaics, and classical-style pillars with elegant stone capitals. Perhaps there were also courtyards, one housing a garden as at Machaerus. Also as at Machaerus, a visitor might have fancied himself in a great house in Rome, but the Jewish prohibition on images of people or animals would have meant that Antipas was looking at geometrical, plant-based or floral patterns on his walls and floors. A Roman visitor might have missed the images of animals, gods, goddesses and people that featured in the frescos and mosaics of Gentile houses in, say, Pompeii.

Antipas's Jerusalem house would no doubt also have had stone vessels full of water for ritual cleaning, similar to those that unexpectedly found themselves full of the best wine at a certain marriage at Cana. Other Jewish features would have included at least one mikva, a ritual bath for the whole body, as well as conventional bathing facilities after the Roman model.

5. Tiberias

It is possible that Antipas's distaste for Pilate, which, according to Luke, was mysteriously cured by their mutual experience of Jesus, was based on the objections the Jews in general had against this particular Roman prefect. According to the Jewish philosopher Philo of Alexandria, who was a contemporary of Pilate's, the prefect had tried to decorate his Jerusalem house with plaques or shields bearing his name and that of the emperor Tiberius. Although the plaques had no graven images on them that would have offended the Second Commandment, the local Jews still objected to them, and a delegation was sent to Pilate to remonstrate. It is highly likely that Antipas was a member of this delegation, and the frosty meeting or meetings it undoubtedly led to may have been a source for Pilate and Antipas's mutual dislike.

Antipas might have been particularly affronted by the plaques because Pilate's Jerusalem palace was the old palace of Herod the Great – his father's house. It may be that Antipas hoped that one day political changes would allow him to occupy that house again as King of the Jews. In this context, he may have seen the installation of the plaques as the beginning of a wholesale redecoration of the palace in the Roman style, which would have meant that he would have had to spend a fortune making it Jewish again if he ever moved back in.

Pilate also offended Jewish sensibilities by having Roman military standards with graven images on them brought into Jerusalem, when previous prefects had only used standards that had been specially adapted so as not to offend the Jewish ban on the depiction of people or animals. This also might have offended Antipas.

Even when he was trying to show the locals what wonderful things the Romans could do for them, Pilate offended the Jews. When he built a much-needed aqueduct for Jerusalem, there were mass protests because he had funded this project by using the sacred money of the Temple. Depending on exactly when these events happened in relation to each other, Antipas might have joined in these protests, but harboured a secret sympathy for the prefect's efforts. He too fell foul of Jewish sensibilities when he built his new city of Tiberias on the west coast of the Sea of Galilee. Tiberias, which was named after the Roman emperor Tiberius, was founded by Antipas around 20 CE, in what many regard as the most beautiful part of Galilee, on the site of the ancient village of Rakkath. The area was already famous for one of its most inviting features – hot springs that were said to have medicinal benefits for bathers, which Josephus tells us were located nearby at Emmaus, a place familiar to readers of the gospels. These hot springs seem to have given Tiberias something of the character of a spa town in Europe, such as Bath in England or Baden-Baden in Germany. It is likely that, with its special waters, the local bath-house in Tiberias could offer something better than the run-of-the-mill bath-houses of the Roman world.

As in medieval times, and during the eighteenth and nineteenth centuries in Europe, the health benefits of bathing in waters said to have special properties were firmly believed in in first-century Palestine. Herod the Great, Antipas's father, sought a cure for the various horrible health problems that afflicted him in later life by bathing in the waters at Calirrhoe on the east coast of the Dead Sea.

185

Bathing in oil was another cure attempted on Herod the Great, but since his main problem was probably kidney disease it is unlikely that any kind of bathing could have done him much good.

His new city of Tiberias became Antipas's headquarters, and the capital of Galilee, and here he built houses for the future settlers, and set aside plots of land for many of them to use to grow fruit and vegetables. Antipas moved the archives (probably meaning the 'high court') of the Herodian ruling family there from the city of Sepphoris, and built himself a splendid palace with gold ceilings and fine paintings – perhaps frescos – on the walls. There was also a stadium and a huge synagogue, a grand gate at the southern entrance to the city, a large basilica, buildings with high-quality marble floors, walls and pillars covered in smooth plaster and painted to look like marble, and a *cardo* or paved main street. In 2005, the remains of a beautiful multi-coloured marble floor made using a technique called *opus sectile* were also found by archaeologists.

Later witnesses suggest that Tiberias was ruled by a council of five hundred, from whose number a superior group of ten elders would be chosen. Chief among the duties of these officials would have been the levying of taxes. The city's hierarchy was distinctly Greek in character, and various dignitaries bore Greek titles such as 'agronomos', 'archon' and 'hyparch'.

An unwary time-traveller wandering into the city of Tiberias during the first century CE might mistake it for a Roman or perhaps a Greek city, not least because of the nature of its ruling group; and the construction of a stadium in particular would suggest that Antipas was trying to introduce elements of the Roman life-style to his new city, where it is thought that most of the citizens in his day would have been Jewish. In the stadium, which seems to have been big enough to hold tens of thousands of spectators, the usual Roman-style gladiatorial combats might have been staged, as well as musical and athletic events, horse-races, and the hideous spectacles during which prisoners condemned to death would be fed to hungry wild animals.

In his exhaustive book on Herod Antipas, Morten Hørning Jensen suggests that such types of entertainment could have been made more palatable to the Jewish locals by removing specifically Pagan elements from them. Examples of features that might have offended Jewish spectators would have been the officials dressed as the Pagan gods Mercury and Charon who took part in gladiatorial combats. To ensure that a fallen gladiator was not faking death, 'Mercury' was sometimes ordered to poke him with a hot iron rod, and 'Charon' would be called upon to 'finish off' wounded gladiators with a mallet.

Even if none of the Jewish locals appreciated the entertainments staged in the Tiberias stadium, the shows might have drawn in local Gentiles, and would probably have served the purpose of honouring Antipas's masters among the Roman ruling family. Games were routinely staged in honour of Roman emperors and their relatives, and such gestures would no doubt have been noted and appreciated far away in Rome.

The Roman character of Tiberias is supposed to have extended to the nature of the aforementioned decorations on the walls of Antipas's palace there. Whereas, as we have seen, similar palaces in the holy city of Jerusalem at this time tended to be decorated with geometrical or plant-based designs, it seems that the pictures in the Tiberias palace transgressed the Jewish religious laws against the depiction of people and animals. As a result, the palace was burned down during the Jewish revolt that led to the Jewish war against the Romans towards the end of the first century. During part of this conflict, the Jewish historian Josephus came to know Tiberias in his role of governor of Galilee. By this time there were synagogues, a basilica or assembly-hall, Pagan temples and a defensible castle there.

The problem with structures at Tiberias such as the grand buildings mentioned above, which have been explored by archaeologists and which eye-witnesses described, is that we cannot be sure whether they were built by Antipas during his time as tetrarch of Galilee and Perea. The same is true of the Greek-style administration with its 'archons' and 'hyparchs': did it exist when Antipas was tetrarch? Tiberias enjoyed its greatest days much later than Antipas's time, and as a result many fine later buildings were constructed atop first-century structures, obliterating them, and in some cases re-using stones cut for different purposes in the first century.

In any case, however far Antipas got with the building of his fine new city, he felt sufficiently proud of it to issue coins bearing the name of Tiberias, though he was not usually a particularly enthusiastic issuer of currency. It may be significant that Antipas's Tiberias coins do not bear images of grand buildings in the city, as later coins issued there did, but merely plant-based decorations such as wreaths, and what have been identified as reeds; the latter perhaps referring to the city's lakeside setting.

Although Antipas's new city was magnificent, or was intended to be magnificent, in his time, and although its setting was inviting, Josephus implies that many local Jews were reluctant to settle there because at least part of Tiberias had been built on top of old Jewish graves.

Jewish religious law dictated that anyone who came into the slightest contact with the remains of a dead person would be ritually unclean for seven days. To become impure in this way meant that one's activities could be severely restricted: people who touched an impure person would themselves become impure, as would items such as drinking-vessels that the impure person used. These regulations are detailed in the Old Testament Book of Numbers (19: 11-16).

As a result of Tiberias's alleged impurity, many Jews, particularly priests, preferred to avoid the city altogether, and even went round it rather than passing through. How, then, was Antipas to populate his new city? The Tetrarch resorted to the tyrannical practices typical of his dynasty, and forced many Jews from Galilee to live there – even high-status Jews who would presumably have helped to form the upper class, some of the men sitting on Tiberias's ruling council.

There was also an influx of Gentiles attracted by the Tetrarch's offer of houses and land, and not put off by the threat of Jewish ritual impurity, that would have meant nothing to them. These willing Gentile settlers, and unwilling Jews, were still not enough to make up the population of a great city, so Antipas imported numbers of poor people, desperate for anywhere to live. He also invited large numbers of slaves, who were promised their freedom if only they swore in turn that they would stay in the city. In the words of the 1906 *Jewish Encyclopaedia*, the Tetrarch was 'obliged to induce beggars, adventurers, and foreigners to come [to Tiberias]; and in some cases he had even to use violence to carry out his will'.

The ritual impurity of the city of Tiberias seems to have continued to be a concern until the end of the first century and even into the second. It was then that a Jewish sage, Rabbi Simeon ben Yohai, decided to do the city a favour by purifying it and removing its ritual taint.

Rabbi Simeon felt grateful to Tiberias because himself and his son, who was also a rabbi, had been cured of identical skin problems after bathing in the city's celebrated waters. Their respective skins had broken out in sores after they had lived in a cave for years, drinking fresh water from a nearby spring and eating carobs. It is likely that they had been hiding in their cave to avoid persecution as Jews under the Romans.

Before he could purify the city, which he did at the suggestion of his son, the good rabbi had to get the agreement of the local Jewish religious hierarchy, who voted that he should be allowed to go ahead. What happened next is related differently in different accounts: my version is a conflation of these.

Rabbi Simeon literally brought the human corpses under Tiberias to light by throwing lupins on the ground above them. This made the old bones come to the surface: they could then be carried away and re-buried elsewhere. When the rabbi announced that all the city's corpses had been removed in this way, a man, who is described as a Samaritan in some sources, tried to prove Simeon wrong by pointing out that in one place there was a corpse still left under the ground. The rabbi immediately realised that the Samaritan had deliberately hidden a new corpse there, and the would-be trickster died instantly.

On his way home through a place called Migdal Zevaaya, Rabbi Simeon encountered a man called Nikaia the scribe. Nikaia also foolishly raised the question of whether the rabbi had managed to remove all of the corpses; and he was punished with a deadly snake-bite.

Thus cleansed by the indomitable Rabbi Simeon ben Yohai, Tiberias, the city Antipas had founded, went on to become a leading centre of Jewish religion, scholarship and culture. Ironically, given its early reputation for ritual impurity derived from corpses, the city's necropolis became a popular place for high-status burials. Coffins were transported there from many miles away so that the pious Jews inside them could rest in such a revered place.

In his detailed account of the purification of Tiberias (see the Hebrew Union College Annual, Vol. 49 (1978)) Lee Levine suggests that Josephus may have emphasised the ritual impurity of the city because he had had a poor experience of the place during the Jewish War, and had come to despise its citizens. Levine also suggests that the impurity story was perpetuated by the people of the rival Galilean city of Sepphoris, which is west of Tiberias and less than four miles north of Nazareth.

Before Antipas moved his treasury and archives to Tiberias, Sepphoris had been both his headquarters and the capital of Galilee. The people of Sepphoris naturally resented the way that the upstart city on the Sea of Galilee had usurped their place, albeit temporarily; and they were keen to raise any objections to Tiberias that they could. In response, suggests Levine, the Tiberians cooked up their own story of how their city had been purified by a miracle-working rabbi, who was not to be crossed: in a story that is often attached to the Tiberias purification account, a man suggests that Rabbi Simeon had approved an action that was against Jewish religious law, and the angry sage caused the man to collapse into a heap of bare bones.

Levine suggests that, if indeed they made up the story of Rabbi Simeon's purification of their city, the Tiberians may have based it on an older Pagan Greek story concerning the philosopher Epimenides. Like Rabbi Simeon, Epimenides had spent time living in a cave – in his case as long as fifty-seven years. When he emerged, the Athenians begged the philosopher to purify their city, which he did via a series of procedures including the removal of human bones. The similarities between the stories of Epimenides and Rabbi Simeon hint at the links between Greco-Roman and Jewish culture that were bound to be forged when Galilee was home to so many Gentiles, and had been dominated by both the Greeks and later the Romans.

6. Sepphoris

Since Tiberias had only been a village before Antipas began to build his new city on the site, the tetrarch could justifiably claim it as a new city. This was not the case with Sepphoris, which had been a considerable city, but needed re-building in Antipas's time because it was supposed to have been utterly destroyed by the Romans, and its people sold into slavery.

In the gap between the death of Herod the Great around 4 BCE and the re-organisation of his territories by the Romans under his sons and his sister Salome, various rebel movements had risen up, hoping to fill the power vacuum and establish a new dynasty. Josephus tells us that there were more than ten thousand rebellions in Judea alone: one of these involved some two thousand soldiers from Herod the Great's army, which had been disbanded. These men rose up and managed to prevail against the forces of Herod's first cousin, Achiabus, whom they drove into the mountains.

Gratus, a high-ranking officer in Herod the Great's army, had more success against one Simon, who had been a slave of Herod's. As if to prove that, even two thousand years ago, tall, good-looking people enjoyed certain advantages, Simon inspired loyalty among many people when he presumed to crown himself king, and set about burning and plundering Herodian cities and palaces. Gratus raised an army against Simon's rebels, and met them in battle with his combined force of Roman soldiers and local troops. After a hard fight, the superior skill and experience of Gratus's men began to tell against the enthusiastic but poorly-organised rebels. The tall, handsome Simon tried to make good his escape – but Gratus managed to intercept him and cut off his head.

Another rebel leader of this time was Athronges, a shepherd. Josephus does not tell us that he was handsome like the ill-fated Simon, but he and his four warlike brothers were tall and strong, and established a powerful junta for themselves that lasted for some time. Eventually this movement was suppressed by Gratus and his troops, together with Archelaus, Herod's the Great's son and a full brother to Antipas, and also Ptolemy, a friend of the late king's.

The time was so lawless that the whole area became dangerous and chaotic, crime flourished and it must have been hard, at times, to distinguish rebels from mere robbers. Josephus is clear that some of those who attacked the Romans, Herod the Great's troops and the Herodian cities, were partly motivated by their memories of how they had suffered under these rulers, and by the dream of an independent Jewish state with no Herods in charge. But Josephus is also clear that many of the rebels were simply motivated by greed for plunder, lust for power, and the enjoyment of murder, mayhem and destruction.

It is possible that another rebel of this time, Judas son of Ezekias, was concerned to found an independent *republic* for the Jews, although Josephus insists that this man, whom he describes as the vicious leader of a band of profligates, also wanted to become a king. Judas managed to invade the strongly fortified city of Sepphoris, empty the armoury of the palace there, and make off with all the money from the treasury. It is also possible that the Ezekias or Hezekiah who was the father of this Judas was the founder of the Zealot movement of patriotic rebels which had sprung up in Galilee over forty years earlier.

The senior Roman in Judea during the aftermath of Herod the Great's death was probably Sabinus, who had been sent there by the Roman emperor Augustus to take charge of Herod the Great's estates after the latter's death. Unable to cope with the violent and chaotic situation, Sabinus wrote for help to Publius Quinctilius Varus, who was then the Roman Governor of Syria. In response to Sabinus's plea, Varus set off for Judea with two legions, partly because he was concerned about the fate of his third legion. This legion was already on the ground, and may have been under threat, out of its depth and in need of support.

Varus supplemented his two legions with four troops of horsemen; and various rulers in the region also supplied him with auxiliaries. These allies included Aretas, king of the Nabateans, a groups of Arabs whose lands bordered what was to become Antipas's territory of Perea, to the east of the Jordan. Perea included the aforementioned fortress of Machaerus, where Antipas later had John the Baptist beheaded.

It was during Varus's campaign that troops under his generals destroyed the city of Sepphoris and sold its citizens into slavery. Eventually Varus brought the region back under Roman control, though not before his Nabatean allies had caused a great deal of mayhem. Varus himself is thought to have crucified two thousand rebels.

Although he played a crucial role in 'pacifying' the region after the death of Herod the Great, Publius Quinctilius Varus is also remembered today as the Roman governor of Germania who marched three legions into an ambush in the Teutoberg Forest, east of modern Osnabrück in north-west Germany, in the September of 9 CE. This was recorded as one of the greatest disasters the Roman army ever suffered: the shame of utter defeat led Varus to kill himself.

When Herod Antipas was eventually allowed to become a puppet leader for the Romans in Galilee, he set about re-building Sepphoris.

Because Sepphoris is just an hour's walk away from Nazareth, where Jesus grew up, commentators have long speculated on how this major building project might have impacted on the boyhood of Christ. Might he have played among the building-sites of the city, climbing on its new defensive wall as it was being erected? Could it be that he was born in Bethlehem because his parents lived there at the time, and did his father Joseph move the family to Nazareth in order to take up work among the builders of the new Sepphoris?

According to the Gospels, Jesus did not begin his ministry until he was around thirty years of age, after he was baptised by John the Baptist. In his teens and twenties, did he work with his father and brother James as a carpenter on the new buildings that were going up in Sepphoris? Did his time in Antipas's new city allow him to mix with different sorts of people, unlike those he could expect to encounter in a conservative, very Jewish sort of place like Nazareth? Did Nazareth seem to him like an enclave of traditional Judaism, while Sepphoris, by contrast, introduced him to new ways of thinking? Was Sepphoris where he learned Greek and perhaps Latin, and met with Greek and Roman Pagans, and also with Samaritans, and Arabs from the south and east? Could it be that Antipas's project to re-build Sepphoris inadvertently helped to enrich the later message of Jesus?

The historian and New Testament scholar John Dominic Crossan has put forward the idea that during his encounters on the streets of Sepphoris, Jesus heard about various religious and philosophical views that would have contrasted with the traditional Judaism he found at home, only an hour's walk away. Among the diverse philosophical schools to be found among the Greeks, who in those days were spread all over the Mediterranean area, was the Cynical philosophy associated with figures like the philosophers Antisthenes and Diogenes: the latter died in

Corinth in 323 BCE.

The more extreme Cynical philosophers, whose name meant 'dog-like', gave up any wealth they had, and embraced poverty and homelessness, dressing in a few coarse clothes and sometimes owning nothing but a small bag of possessions and a staff. Today we might compare them to the aghori, ascetic holy men of India. Diogenes himself destroyed his wooden bowl when he saw a boy drinking from his cupped hands – the sight made him realise that he didn't even need a bowl. He lived in a barrel or large ceramic pot in the street, and was an outspoken critic of the Greek society on the outer fringe of which he lived much of his life. He carried a lit lamp around in broad daylight, claiming that he was looking for an honest man, spat or urinated on people he disapproved of, defecated in the theatre and even masturbated in public.

In his 2012 book on the archaeological evidence for Jesus, Craig A. Evans pours a lot of cold water on the Jesus as Cynic idea, pointing out that in the gospel passages where Jesus sometimes sounds like a Cynical philosopher, he is often saying the complete opposite of what the Cynics typically said. Whereas the Cynics were recognisable as what they were because of their bags, coarse cloaks and staffs, Jesus specifically advised his followers to travel *without* a bag or staff:

When Jesus had called the Twelve together, he gave them power and authority to drive out all demons and to cure diseases, and he sent them out to proclaim the kingdom of God and to heal the sick. He told them: "Take nothing for the journey—no staff, no bag, no bread, no money, no extra shirt . . . "

(Lk 9:1-3)

Evans also draws on archaeological evidence that suggests that, at least before the disastrous war between the Jews and the Romans that ended around 70 CE, Sepphoris was home to nothing like the multi-faith, cosmopolitan community some have assumed lived there.

In the city's rubbish-dump, no pig's bones are found lower than the 70 CE level; which indicates an entirely Jewish population, who were all observing the ancient dietary restrictions at least to the extent that they were avoiding pork. The Sepphoris rubbish-dump also contained broken vessels, made of stone and ceramic, of typically Jewish types. Evans explains that, because of fear of ritual contamination, observant Jews at this time would not buy or use Gentile pottery, and preferred to use stone vessels where possible, despite the fact that they were heavy, expensive and hard to make: it was thought to be more difficult for stone vessels to become ritually unclean.

Another sign that Sepphoris, at least before around 70 CE, had a majority Jewish population, is the large numbers of mikva'ot that archaeologists have unearthed there. These ritual baths are distinctively Jewish, and quite different from ancient bath-tubs used for ordinary washing. In fact, among the remains of some Jewish houses from the first century, archaeologists have found conventional baths similar to those found in houses all over the world today, that seem to have been placed in such a way that it would be easy for the users to wash themselves before entering the separate mikvah or Jewish ritual bath.

As for the other architectural remains found at Sepphoris, there seems to be even less here that can be ascribed with certainty to Antipas as a builder than there is at Tiberias. It may be that the theatre, or an early version of it, was built during the reign of Antipas and also during the youth of Jesus, and it is possible that knowledge, or even direct experience, of the dramas staged at Sepphoris informed Jesus' message. He sometimes speaks about various types of 'hypocrites', whom he often asserts will be sorely punished for their crimes by God. A typical passage is this one from the Gospel of Matthew:

Woe to you, teachers of the law and Pharisees, you hypocrites! You are like whitewashed tombs, which look beautiful on the outside but on the inside are full of the bones of the dead and everything unclean. In the same way, on the outside you appear to people as righteous but on the inside you are full of hypocrisy and wickedness.

(Mt 23:27-8)

The Greek word from which our English word 'hypocrite' is derived is a word for a dissembler or pretender, but it can also refer to an actor. If he had knowledge of what went on in his nearby theatre, the young Jesus might have seen this as a symbol for certain types of harmful pretence and dissembling that he saw in real life, and was eager to condemn, especially when he witnessed this behaviour among the richest, most powerful, influential and respected members of his own Jewish community.

Like modern actors, ancient Greek-style actors wore costumes appropriate to the characters they were supposed to be representing; but they also wore masks to completely transform their appearance. This was handy when it came to the female characters, since, as in Shakespeare's theatre, women were not allowed to act in public.

Greek-style actors also wore built-up shoes so that they would appear taller; spoke lines written for them by someone else (saying things they would never have the need to say in real life) and simulated emotions that they did not really feel. Jesus might therefore have been thinking of these paradoxical creatures, the actors, when he criticised the 'teachers of the law and Pharisees'. According to Jesus, these people put on a good appearance but were bad inside, deliberately looking sad when they were fasting, so that everyone knew that they were fasting (Mt 6:16). They also wore large phylacteries and long tassels on their garments as a kind of misleading costume, to help them seem more holy (Mt 23:5).

It is possible that by comparing the hypocrites he saw among the Pharisees and the teachers of the law to actors, Jesus was implying some criticism of the acting profession itself. If so, he would not have been the first. In his *Republic*, the Greek philosopher Plato, who died around 347 BCE, argued that there would be no room for actors in the ideal state, which he thought would be characterised by simplicity and honesty. He believed that actors' own characters could be adversely affected by the traits of the characters they portrayed – the mask becoming the actor's real face – and he disliked the idea that actors might portray worse men than they were themselves. He was particularly scornful of the idea of men playing women:

We cannot allow men to play the parts of women, quarrelling, weeping, scolding, or boasting against the gods, — least of all when making love or in labour. They must not represent slaves, or bullies, or cowards, drunkards, or madmen, or blacksmiths, or neighing horses, or bellowing bulls, or sounding rivers, or a raging sea. A good or wise man will be willing to perform good and wise actions, but he will be ashamed to play an inferior part . . .

If Jesus was thinking about the actors of Sepphoris when he spoke about hypocrites, he may have been thinking about the look of the place from a distance when he talked about 'a town built on a hill' that 'cannot be hidden', a metaphor he used to describe the spiritual light he sensed in his disciples. In this passage, he goes on to say:

Neither do people light a lamp and put it under a bowl. Instead they put it on its stand, and it gives light to everyone in the house. In the same way, let your light shine before others, that they may see your good deeds and glorify your Father in heaven.

(Mt 5:15-16)

When he said this, was he thinking about the city of Sepphoris at night or before dawn on its hill, with its lights and fires glowing? Did he see this sight as he went to or came from working on the city with his father and brother?

7. Decline and Fall

We have seen how Aretas, king of the Nabateans, lent troops to Quintillius Varus when he came to suppress the various revolts that sprang up in the Holy Land following the death of Herod the Great. Although it seems that the troops he lent to the Romans got seriously out of hand, sacking and looting the territory of their old enemies the Jews, Aretas, who was actually the fourth Nabatean king of that name, was evidently a useful ally; and when Herod Antipas took possession of Galilee and Perea, he married Aretas's daughter Phasaelis. Nabatea bordered Antipas's territory of Perea in what is now Jordan, which made the alliance particularly useful for Antipas.

Strategic considerations seem to have gone right out of Antipas's head, however, when he visited his older half-brother, another Herod, in Rome. This Herod, known as Herod II or Herod Philip, was the son of Herod the Great's second wife, who was also his second wife to be called Mariamne. Herod Philip's wife when Antipas visited him was Herodias, who, in keeping with the dynasty's tradition of in-breeding, was also his half-niece. Herodias had borne her first husband a daughter, Salome, who, as we have seen, may have been the girl who danced before Herod Antipas and, prompted by her mother, demanded the head of John the Baptist as payment.

To complicate the family tree still further, during his

time in his half-brother's house in Rome, Antipas fell in love with Herodias, who was not only his half sister-in-law but also his own half-niece. Soon negotiations were under way for Antipas to marry Herodias: to do this, he was required to divorce his wife Phasaelis, the daughter of Aretas IV Philopatris, King of the Nabateans.

Antipas neglected to tell his Arabian wife of many years about their upcoming divorce, but she soon heard about it, and asked to be transferred to the aforementioned castle of Machaerus in Perea, east of the Dead Sea. From there it was an easy matter for her to be conducted by some of her father's generals back home to nearby Nabatea.

The capital of the Nabateans' territory, to which Phasaelis would surely have been taken at this time, was the so-called 'rose-red city' of Petra, an extraordinary artificial oasis in the desert that survived because of the Nabateans' ability to capture and store water from the torrential rains that occasionally visited this otherwise parched area. Their water supply secured, the citizens of Petra were able to sit back and enjoy the revenues that rolled in as a result of their control over the trade-routes that criss-crossed the desert.

Today, Petra, which was not 'rediscovered' by the West until 1812, is a UNESCO world heritage site, and far and away the biggest tourist attraction in the modern state of Jordan. Here visitors can see elaborate tombs cut into the living rock of narrow canyons. These resemble ancient temples and tombs built from the ground up by more conventional means, such as are to be seen at Jerusalem and elsewhere, but they are the result of highly-skilled carving, and not construction. The finest of these, the so-called 'Treasury', is thought to date from the time of Antipas, Phasaelis and her father King Aretas IV.

With his spurned daughter safely at home, Aretas IV set about making war against Antipas, with whom he already had a disagreement concerning the precise location of the borders of a place called Gamalitis. According to Josephus,

Antipas's army was destroyed in the subsequent war, partly because some of his troops went over to Aretas's side.

Josephus gives no details of this battle, but it is not surprising that the Nabateans won. If they managed to lure Antipas's force out into the desert, then their victory was assured. Few armies could survive for long in this dessicated environment, but the Nabateans knew the lie of the land, and had knowledge of hidden supplies of water. There are accounts of their leading enemy forces out into the desert, then just waiting for them to surrender. It may be that the men from Antipas's army who defected to the Nabatean side did so because Aretas promised them water, and safe conduct back home.

Antipas's expedition led to the military defeat which, Josephus reports, many at the time identified as a punishment from God imposed on Antipas because he had killed John the Baptist.

No doubt severely rattled by his defeat, and licking his metaphorical wounds, Antipas begged for help from Rome. In response, the emperor Tiberius ordered Vitellius, the then governor of Syria, to intervene with his own troops.

As Vitellius was marching through Judea with two Roman legions and numbers of local auxiliaries, the Jewish authorities intercepted him and begged him not to march on on his intended route, because his army's standards bore graven images that offended their religious sensibilities. Vitellius politely sent his army on a different route, while he himself joined Antipas for a festival in Jerusalem. After a few days, news came that the emperor Tiberius had died, and been replaced by his nephew Gaius, the notorious emperor known to history by his childhood nick-name, Caligula. Although Vitellius had instructions from the late Tiberius to proceed against the Nabateans, he had none from Caligula, so he called off his campaign.

The death of Tiberius in 37 CE was to have even more serious consequences for Herod Antipas. Shortly after

Caligula, Tiberius's nephew, became emperor, he released another Herod, Herod Agrippa, from prison where, it must be said, he had been having a rather comfortable time because of the various privileges he had been granted. Agrippa was a grandson of Herod the Great, whom Tiberius had had locked up because of a foolish thing he had said one day to his friend Caligula when they were out riding in Agrippa's chariot together in Rome. He told Caligula that he wished Tiberius would soon die, so that he, Caligula, could become emperor, since he was much more worthy of the office.

Agrippa's words were overheard by the driver of the chariot, one Eutychus, who was a freedman of Agrippa's. Eutychus would never have reported these dangerous words to anyone, except that Agrippa later accused him of stealing some of his clothes: Josephus, who rather admired Herod Agrippa, tells us that Eutychus certainly had stolen the garments in question. Thus accused, Eutychus ran away from his master. When he was caught, he said to Piso, the governor of Rome, who was acting as a magistrate, that he had something important to say to Tiberius. When at last the emperor, who was a terrible procrastinator, had heard Eutychus out, Agrippa was arrested and sent to prison.

As Agrippa was leaning on a tree, waiting to be carted off to prison, another prisoner, evidently a German clairvoyant, told him through an interpreter that he, Agrippa, would see better times, but that when he saw another owl like the one that was in the tree above them, he would soon die.

On the succession of Caligula, Agrippa was quickly released. He seems to have had a gift for making and keeping valuable friends: the most valuable ones he ever made were undoubtedly Caligula and his successor as emperor, Claudius. Caligula not only released Agrippa: he had him brought to his own palace, where he was shaved, given new clothes, and had a crown put on his head. The new emperor also gave Agrippa a gold chain equal in weight to the iron one he had been forced to wear in prison. He was then given the tetrarchy that had been left vacant on the death of his uncle Philip the Tetrarch, as well as a small additional territory that had been controlled by one Lysanias. The former comprised a large area to the north and east of Antipas's Galilee.

When Agrippa went east to claim his tetrarchy, the sight of his new-found wealth, power and success deeply offended his sister Herodias, Antipas's wife. She was particularly upset because Agrippa had spent so many years as a shiftless bankrupt, and had even relied on charity from his brother-in-law Antipas to stay afloat at all. Herodias insisted that her husband should proceed to Rome and try his own luck with the new emperor, thinking perhaps that if he did so, he might be made a king and she herself a queen. Antipas resisted her words for a long time, but was finally brought round. He made preparations for a luxurious trip to Italy for himself and Herodias, and soon met Caligula at the imperial spa town of Baiae on the Gulf of Naples.

Agrippa had, however, heard about Antipas's travel plans, and had sent his freedman Fortunatus to deliver his own letters straight to the emperor. These arrived while Antipas was with Caligula, and when the emperor read them he found that they were full of accusations designed to make him see his visitor in a very poor light. Antipas, Agrippa wrote, had conspired with Tiberius's enemy Sejanus when he was alive, and was now plotting against Rome with the king of Parthia, Artabanus. To prove that this accusation was true, Agrippa mentioned a stash of arms and armour, sufficient for seventy thousand men, that Antipas had salted away. When asked directly, Antipas could not deny the existence of this cache, and when Caligula took this as damning evidence of his guilt, Antipas was stripped of his tetrarchy and his wealth (which were given to Agrippa) and banished to Lyon in what is now France. Unfortunately,

Josephus presents Antipas's sudden fall as evidence of what a bad idea it is to listen to the advice of a woman.

Although Josephus does not tell us about any such defence, Antipas could surely have defended himself against the accusations of Agrippa, which had arrived in such an untimely manner in the form of a letter. Any contact Antipas may have had with Lucius Aelius Sejanus must have ended eight years earlier, in 31 CE, when Sejanus was strangled on the orders of the Roman senate, and his body thrown onto the Gemonian stairs in Rome. By that time, Sejanus had become such a notorious public enemy that the Roman mob were only too keen to tear his corpse to pieces.

Sejanus, who, like Pontius Pilate, was from the equestrian or knightly class, was prefect of the Praetorian Guard, the emperor's personal body-guard. Reaching far beyond his class and position, this ambitious man, who probably had a hand in the appointment of Pilate as Prefect of Judea, became one of the most powerful men in the empire while the vicious, perverted emperor Tiberius frittered away his time at his island retreat of Capri.

When he was at the height of his power, pretty much everybody in authority in the empire had to work with Sejanus, but we cannot know if Antipas was privy to any plans of his to, for instance, do away with Tiberius and become emperor himself. In fact it is far from clear that Sejanus ever entertained such plans.

If Antipas offered any such arguments in his own defence that day at Baiae, it is likely that they would have fallen on deaf ears: Herod Agrippa was Caligula's trusted friend, and his letters no doubt meant more to him than any speech of Antipas's.

Because Herodias was Agrippa's sister, Caligula was prepared to let her keep her personal wealth after her husband had been stripped of his, but she preferred to share Antipas's misfortune and go into exile with him.

Although Caligula's treatment of his visitors from the

east was perhaps biased and ill-informed, it did not bear any of the hallmarks of the murderous madness he exhibited at other times. Although he may have reduced them to something that would have felt like poverty to them before he packed them off to Gaul, he did not kill them, as he did so many others, often for trivial or whimsical reasons.

It was at Baiae, where he met Antipas and Herodias, that Caligula gave evidence of the sometime bizarre shape of his thought-processes by building a three-mile-long pontoon of ships, weighted with sand and joined together with planks, to make a wide road from Baiae itself to the mole of Puteoli. He rode up and down this marine road for two days in striking costumes, supposedly to challenge an old prophecy that he had as much chance of becoming emperor as he had of riding across that particular stretch of water on a horse.

At Lyon, known to the Romans as Lugdunum, to which city Antipas and Herodias were banished, Caligula also embraced an early form of surrealism during some games he staged, which included competitions in Greek and Latin oratory. Here the losers had to present the prizes to the winners, give speeches in praise of them and either erase their own efforts with sponges or their own tongues, or be thrashed and thrown into one of the city's rivers. Also at Lugdunum, Caligula staged a rigged auction of furniture brought from the imperial palace in Rome. The auction was rigged because specific citizens had been told in advance what to buy and how much to pay. This was an indicator of what would become a disturbingly prominent feature of Caligula's short-lived regime – empty imperial coffers. Later, the emperor would turn part of his palace in Rome into a brothel to raise funds.

Although that particular visit from the emperor must have been unnerving, Lugdunum or Roman Lyon seems not to have been the wretched backwater to which one might have expected Caligula to banish people whom he believed had been plotting against him. It was a thriving city of perhaps over one hundred thousand people, with many of the typical Roman amenities, including both a theatre and an amphitheatre, temples and a mint. Two emperors, Claudius and Caracalla, were born there, and as well as the visit from Caligula, Lugdunum played host to the emperor Augustus on several occasions. The city was an important commercial, strategic and administrative centre, but even with modern global warming, the mean temperature in winter here is just above three degrees centigrade – nearly seven degrees lower than the January average at Jerusalem.

According to a late apocryphal text called The Letter of Herod to Pilate, a particularly cold snap, presumably at Lyons, brought tragedy to Antipas's family. His daughter Herodias was playing on the ice when she fell in up to her neck. His wife, also called Herodias of course, tried to pull the girl out, but the sharp ice severed the girl's head completely, while the rest of her body was swept away under the ice by the strong current.

Antipas is supposedly writing his letter to Pilate while his wife, who has gone blind in one eye from weeping, is cradling the dead girl's head, no doubt intended, in this story, to be an ironic reminder of the head of John the Baptist, which Herodias had once coveted. Antipas's son Lesbonax is also dying, and he himself has dropsy and live worms coming out of his mouth. In the letter, Herod is quite clear that these afflictions have come to his family because of his crimes regarding Jesus and John the Baptist. The author of this pious fraud also has Herod feeling racked with guilt about the Massacre of the Innocents – for which Herod the Great, not Herod Antipas, was responsible, supposing that that atrocity ever actually took place.

The fact is that with their exile to Gaul Antipas and Herodias stepped behind the curtain of history: we can only speculate on what happened to them during their time at the city on the confluence of the Rhône and the Saône. If they lived long enough, they would certainly have heard news of developments in Rome, and in their homeland, in Lugdunum, where four important Roman roads and two major rivers allowed for relatively speedy communication. They probably had the satisfaction of hearing that Caligula, who had rapidly grown cruel and demented after he became emperor, was assassinated in 41 CE.

They might have suspected that Herod Agrippa, who had gained so much power at Caligula's hands, might fall with him, but in fact Agrippa helped secure the next emperor, Claudius, in the imperial throne, because he was in Rome and at the centre of things when Caligula's death created a dangerous power vacuum. The grateful Claudius made Agrippa ruler of Samaria, and also Judea, which had long been ruled by Roman prefects like Pontius Pilate. This made Agrippa, in effect, a second Herod the Great, despite his years as an obscure, bankrupt adventurer, when Antipas had felt obliged to help him out.

Like his grandfather Herod the Great, Agrippa became a great builder and a patron of fine cities. He was also noted for his piety and loyalty to the Jewish religion, and risked his own neck trying to intercede when the insane Caligula, who had become convinced that he personally was a god, hatched a mad scheme to put a large golden statue of himself in the Temple at Jerusalem.

Fine as it was in many ways, Herod Agrippa's reign did not, however, last long. After only seven years, in 44 CE, according to Josephus, he died during some games he was staging in honour of the emperor Claudius at Caesarea Maritima, the port city his grandfather had built. He saw an owl above his head, and, as we know, he had been told years before that when he saw such a bird, it would be the end of him. Needless to say, this type of superstition was quite unacceptable to observant Jews at this time.

The account of Agrippa's death in the New Testament Book of Acts is quite different from Josephus's. In Acts we are told that during a speech he was making at a political conference, people were shouting out that his voice was that of a god, not a mortal. Because of this, he was struck down by an angel and died eaten by worms (Acts 12:23). Interestingly, his grandfather Herod the Great had also been troubled by worms – in his case these creatures ate his gangrenous genitals. It has been suggested that both men may have suffered from something called Fournier's gangrene. Perhaps the traditional in-breeding habits of their family made the Herodians susceptible to certain rare diseases, and more likely to pass them on to succeeding generations than people with a healthy genetic mix.

In Acts, Agrippa's death follows straight on from an account of his persecution of the Christians. He had the apostle James, the brother of John and son of Zebedee, killed, then, seeing that this pleased the local Jews, he had Peter arrested. Peter was, however, rescued from his prison by an angel, who made his chains fall off and caused locked doors to spring open.

8. Ways of Seeing

Although the ban on depicting Biblical characters on the London stage halted rehearsals for the English premier of Oscar Wilde's play *Salome* in 1892, it was only an astonishing five years later that film-makers in the United States and Europe shrugged off such considerations and began to produce screen versions of Biblical stories. An 1897 film called *La Passion du Christ* is now lost, but a French film from 1898 called *La vie et la passion de Jésus-Christ* has not only survived, but can now be watched for free in its entirety via the internet.

There has been no strong tradition of stage depictions of Biblical stories on the English stage in the twentieth and twenty-first centuries, but there have been many films based on various parts of the Bible. Every year, it seems, there are also new television versions of the Passion story, which are usually broadcast in time for Easter.

For film-makers in the silent era, familiar tales from the Bible must have had considerable appeal because most of the audience already knew the story: the story-telling problems that screen-writers for silent movies struggled with every day must have been alleviated by the knowledge that almost everybody out there in the tip-up seats could easily follow what was going on. Biblical films also conferred an air of respectability on studios and the nascent cinema industry in general: they were 'prestige pictures' that often found their way to new audiences who would not usually attend cinemas at all.

Many of the early silent 'Jesus films' are very short, and tend to exclude Herod Antipas and John the Baptist as characters in a sub-plot that is not essential to a brief re-telling of the story of Jesus. Even Cecil B. DeMille's 1927 silent epic *The King of Kings* excludes them, although it is over two hours long, and manages to find time for scenes not to be found in the gospels, such as Jesus repairing a child's doll.

The amount of screen-time DeMille's Mary Magdalen gets is one possible reason why any depiction of Salome would be an unnecessary addition to *The King of Kings*. Since Mary is depicted as a scantily-clad courtesan, this film already has its share of female allure and scandal.

Although it has a similar title, the 1961 feature film *King of Kings*, directed by Nicholas Ray, has a very different plot-line from the silent *The King of Kings*, and does manage to include both the Salome episode and Antipas's later interview with Jesus, as mentioned by Luke. We have already seen how in Pasolini's 1964 film of the Gospel of Matthew, Salome is played by a twelve year-old girl, giving the scene of her dance disturbing overtones of paedophilia. In Ray's film, Salome is played by the seventeen year-old Brigid Bazlen, an actress who was then being heralded as the new Elizabeth Taylor, so that Antipas's sexual interest in her seems a little more normal. Here the tetrarch is played with a sour expression and a grey wig and beard by the Australian actor Frank Thring, then in his thirties but looking like a man in his fifties. In the later scene where Antipas meets Jesus, Salome looks as if she has gone mad and returned to infancy as a result of her involvement in the death of the Baptist.

In the 1961 *King of Kings*, the screen-writer is forced to invent dialogue to pad out the scene where Antipas meets Jesus for the first time. Here, when he has looked closely at

Jesus and decided that no, he cannot be John the Baptist, he asks him to turn a ceramic jug into a gold one, then to start a thunder-storm.

As in Pasolini's film, and the celebrated 1977 TV miniseries *Jesus of Nazareth*, directed by another Italian, Franco Zeffirelli, the John the Baptist/Herod Antipas sub-plot adds variety to *King of Kings*. In Pasolini's film, the squalid scene of the Baptist's execution is followed by a scene where Jesus and his disciples are shown crying for the death of John: a simple, effective and moving way to switch from the sub-plot to the main story, which concerns Jesus and not John.

In *Jesus of Nazareth*, the death of John the Baptist is followed by a scene where John's followers, accompanied by Judas Iscariot, watch the Baptist being buried in an unmarked grave in the desert, and discuss whether they should now attach themselves to Jesus. Zeffirelli insists that these men were Zealots, looking for an effective rebel leader, not a figure like Jesus, who is trying to bring about changes inside people, and not necessarily in their political arrangements.

The cut from Antipas's colourful court to the greys and browns of the desert brings a stimulating sense of contrast to this section of *Jesus of Nazareth*: in the 1973 film of the rock opera *Jesus Christ Superstar* the tone also changes abruptly when Jesus is brought before Antipas. Here the tetrarch is played for laughs by the youngish, chubby Josh Mostel, with afro hair and white Bermuda shorts, surrounded by dancing-girls in brightly-coloured bikinis. His upbeat, sarcastic razzmatazz song, addressed to Jesus, fills the scene and, in stage performances of Rice and Lloyd-Webber's musical, frequently brings the house down.

Antipas's involvement with John the Baptist is spread throughout several scenes in *Jesus of Nazareth*, which are interspersed with other material. Here Salome is played by the then thirty year-old Spanish actress Isabel Mestres, lusted after by the forty-eight year-old Christopher Plummer as Herod Antipas.

Mestres' performance as Salome so impressed a young Spanish film director called Pedro Almodóvar that he cast her in the title role of his film *Salome* in 1978. This short film from the eccentric director of *Women on the Verge of a Nervous Breakdown* (1988) and *Tie Me Up! Tie Me Down!* (1990) puts the character of Salome from the New Testament together with Abraham and Isaac from the Old Testament.

The account of John the Baptist's death in Zeffirelli's *Jesus of Nazareth* borrows some details from Wilde's *Salome*. Here the Baptist, played by Michael York, is imprisoned in a cistern, as in Wilde's version, and his voice is audible from Herod's birthday-party, which disturbs Herod very much. Here Salome also demands that Antipas promise her anything she asks *before* she starts dancing, then shocks him with her demand for John's head after her dance has finished. The dance does not, however, take place on a moon-lit terrace, but during the day-time in a sumptuous hall in the palace.

In *Jesus of Nazareth*, Antipas has dozens of elaborately costumed guests at his rowdy birthday party, but in *King of Kings* (1961) it is a much more modest affair, with Roman guests more in evidence. Rather than dance Wilde's Dance of the Seven Veils, which could turn into a kind of striptease, Brigid Bazlen attends the rather dire little feast in a kind of bikini, and can hardly be expected to remove any more clothing. She looks like a cross between a sultry cheer-leader and a Turkish belly-dancer, which clashes oddly with the otherwise very Ancient Egyptian design elements of the scene.

An effective contrast is made between Bazlen's dark, round-faced Salome and Rita Gam's haughty, glacial Herodias, who reminds one of *Vogue* fashion models from the 1950s. As in many film depictions of the relationship between Herodias and Antipas, there is little sign here of the great love that led them to risk everything to marry, and to stay together in exile.

Herod Antipas features heavily in the 1965 film *The Greatest Story Ever Told*, and indeed José Ferrer's performance as the tetrarch is one of the best things in this sprawling, uneven epic, some versions of which stretch to over four hours. Although Ferrer as Antipas has plenty of scenes with John the Baptist, played by Charlton Heston, *The Greatest Story* does not find time for anything like a full treatment of Salome's dance, and the role of Herodias and her daughter in the death of John the Baptist. Here Herod decides for himself that he must have the Baptist executed, while Salome dances around him in a fantastical costume. While viewers familiar with the gospels might understand this as a vague reference to elements of the gospel account, audiences coming to the story for the first time are surely baffled by this scene.

Of those mentioned above, Pasolini's is the only version that sticks closely to the gospel account of the Salome incident, which is almost excluded altogether from George Stevens' film. In Pasolini's version, no dialogue is added to what we learn from Matthew, and the choice to make Salome very young and Antipas threatening and lecherous counts as interpretation rather than poetic licence.

There is a sense that some of the interpolations other film-makers have added to these stories are part of an attempt to make the gospel narratives conform to the conventions of, for instance, a typical Hollywood film. There must be naturalistic dialogue, that reveals character. There must be clear, comprehensible progress in the story, and comic moments need to be used to break up extended periods of miserable, dark action. People's motives and thought-processes need to be explicit, and there must be both clear 'goodies' and 'baddies', with some characters occupying the middle ground between virtue and villainy.

Because Hollywood films have to sell cinema tickets, they also have to take into account the kinds of expectations that have to be met before the typical movie-goer will commit to a purchase. It has been said that some cinema regulars will want to know 'Who's the guy?' and 'Who's the girl'? The lack of an obvious love-interest throughout the gospels may be one reason why relatively few films have been made of them, despite the enormous significance these stories have in western culture.

At a cruder level, studios often like to have a glamorous female actor somewhere in a film (the 'hot chick'), who can feature in trailers and posters. In the Passion narrative, Mary Magdalen and Salome may be the only characters who can qualify, although the woman taken in adultery, if she is not presumed to be Mary Magdalen herself, can fill this role in at least one scene (see John 8:1-11).

To provide the all-important 'guy', many 'Jesus films' also focus on a central character whom the audience can identify with, through whose eyes they see the action. Sometimes this character is not anybody mentioned in the gospels at all. In the 1961 *King of Kings* 'the guy' is a Roman centurion, called Lucius, played by Ron Randell. In Kevin Reynolds' 2016 film *Risen* the camera follows Joseph Fiennes' character Clavius, this time a Roman tribune, through his experience as witness to the Crucifixion, to his investigation of Jesus' resurrection, to time spent with the Apostles.

Clavius was present at the Crucifixion of Jesus, and a similar character, Marcellus Gallio, played by Richard Burton, finds himself in charge of the Crucifixion in the 1953 film *The Robe*. In the 1959 film of *Ben Hur* 'the guy' is Charlton Heston's character, Judah Ben-Hur, who regularly finds himself on the fringes of the Jesus story (in this film, Pontius Pilate is played by Frank Thring, Antipas in *King of Kings*).

Unfortunately, many of the typical film elements that are

often added to 'Jesus films' are not to be found in the gospels, which were not of course written as film treatments.

Pasolini's *Gospel of Matthew* manages to be faithful to its gospel partly because it ignores many of the conventions film-goers take for granted. Most of the actors in the film were amateurs, and the music was drawn from existing recordings in a number of genres, including classical and world music. In parts, Pasolini's remarkable movie is in effect a silent film. The scene, played entirely without words, where Herodias prepares Salome to dance before her step-father is almost miraculous in its eloquence. Salome seems entirely innocent of the enormity of what she has got herself into, while Herodias is by turns proud of and disturbed by her daughter's beauty, then pitying, then grimly determined to go through with her plan to bring about the death of John the Baptist.

The idea of Salome as a young innocent caught up in something far grimmer than she can imagine is an element in Orson Welles' acclaimed 1941 film *Citizen Kane*. Here the troubled millionaire media mogul Charles Foster Kane, played by Welles himself, is determined to turn his mistress, the nightclub singer Susan Alexander, into an opera star. He has an opera specially written for her, based on the story of Salome, which unfortunately serves only to show up the weakness of Susan's voice and her pitiful acting. The impossible relationship between the original Salome and the older Antipas, which is evoked by the choice of subject for the doomed opera, mirrors Kane's equally ill-fated relationship with the younger Susan, played by Dorothy Comingore. While Susan only wants to have a good time and a comfortable marriage, Kane is locked in a bitter quest to make himself adored and admired by everyone else in the world.

Even where film-makers introduce new characters into New Testament stories, and invent sometimes bizarre and extraneous dialogue and action, screenplays, performances,

217

costumes, settings and indeed every ingredient in the film-makers larder cannot help but make up an *interpretation* of the original stories and their *dramatis personae*, even if the result is crude and clueless.

Since they have to entertain as well as interpret, TV and film directors are not necessarily obliged to arrive at, say, a representation of Herod Antipas that is both compelling and entirely consistent with what can be known about the man. Writers of biographies are, however, obliged to exhibit their ability to make an informed judgement.

Although Zeffirelli's treatment of him draws heavily on Wilde's *Salome*, of the productions mentioned above the Antipas of *Jesus of Nazareth* is perhaps the most consistent with what we can guess about the real Antipas, at least in terms of the character Christopher Plummer strives to convey. With the extra elbow-room conferred by the longer miniseries format, the Canadian can go beyond the hints and suggestions he might have been limited to, if he had had the restricted time on screen that an actor playing Antipas in a ninety-minute feature film might have had to be content with.

Plummer's Antipas is clearly a man at his wits' end. The Gospel of Mark tells us that Herod liked to listen to John the Baptist (Mk 6:20): Plummer's Antipas seems to be so desperate to understand the message of the Baptist that it is as if he thinks his own life depends on it. Plummer's Antipas is also alarmed by the activities of the Zealots, who actually make an unsuccessful assassination attempt on him in the TV *Jesus of Nazareth*.

It is clear that, in this reading, the marriage between Antipas and Herodias has also strayed into a very dark area. Mocking, vindictive, suspicious and scheming, the Italian actress Valentina Cortese's Herodias even suggests releasing the Baptist, but only so that her own agents can track him down and kill him.

The prospect of seeing Salome dance raises a kind of

fever in Plummer's Antipas, but as he watches Isabel Mestres' strange, angular gyrations, it is as if he already knows that his infatuation will only bring more trouble on his head.

In a full-length film or TV miniseries about Antipas, there might be room to show that the pressures on the tetrarch went beyond marital problems, inappropriate desires, fear of rebellion and an inability to grasp the message of John the Baptist. In real life, Antipas seems to have been subjected to pressures from so many different directions that one is tempted to suspect that he might have embraced his exile in Lyon as a welcome escape.

As a puppet ruler for the Romans, Antipas, as he ultimately discovered, was liable to be removed at any time, as his brother Archelaus had been. As a member of the Herodian family, trouble for Antipas was just as likely to come from a close relative as it was from the Romans. While technically Jewish, the Herods were not ethnically the same as many of the Jews they ruled over, and many observant Jews doubted their commitment to the faith. To keep the Jews onside, Herod the Great spent lavishly on the Jerusalem Temple, but the Herods also built Pagan temples and lived lives that were sometimes too luxurious to be truly orthodox in the Jewish sense. As John the Baptist made all too clear, the Herodians' tendency to in-breed was particularly shameful in some Jewish eyes.

As well as the nearby enemies he had to be wary of, Antipas also had to watch the activities of people just over his borders and, in the case of the Decapolis region, people who lived in a kind of geographical sandwich between his territories of Galilee and Perea. As we have seen, the tetrarch's attempts to placate the warlike Nabateans by marrying one of their princesses backfired badly when he fell in love with Herodias and began yet another of his dynasty's marriages between close relatives.

Although some of the screen versions mentioned above

have Antipas showing signs of some deep-set recognition that there was something special about both the Baptist and Jesus, it may be that the real Antipas thought of them, if he thought of them at all in later years, as two more examples of Jewish religious fanatics who seemed bound to cause trouble. If Antipas ever met Jesus at all, then he might not have let him slip through his fingers if he had met him on his home turf, in Galilee or Perea, where there would have been less need for him to respect the prerogative of a Roman prefect.

To Herod Antipas and his dynasty, respect for God and religion probably meant placating the powerful priestly aristocracy of the Jerusalem Temple, and neither Jesus nor John were part of that charmed circle.

Of all the pressures on Antipas, the one that might have weighed most heavily on his mind as he strolled by the rivers at Lyon was the pressure of history. The son of Herod the Great, who had so much wealth and power, and the uncle and predecessor of Herod Agrippa, who wrested what power he had from him and went on to become a kind of Herod the Great reborn, did Antipas feel disappointed and inadequate? If he somehow came to know the reason why Christians remember him today, would he be frustrated to find himself part of a sub-plot to the main story of the gospels, and a cameo player in the drama of Jesus' Passion?

Appendix 1: Antipas and John the Baptist from Josephus, *Jewish Antiquities*, Book 18, trans. Whiston.

Now some of the Jews thought that the destruction of Herod's army came from God as a just punishment of what Herod had done against John, who was called the Baptist.

For Herod had killed this good man, who had commanded the Jews to exercise virtue, righteousness towards one another and piety towards God. For only thus, in John's opinion, would the baptism he administered be acceptable to God, namely, if they used it to obtain not pardon for some sins but rather the cleansing of their bodies, inasmuch as it was taken for granted that their souls had already been purified by justice.

Now many people came in crowds to him, for they were greatly moved by his words. Herod, who feared that the great influence John had over the masses might put them into his power and enable him to raise a rebellion (for they seemed ready to do anything he should advise), thought it best to put him to death. In this way, he might prevent any mischief John might cause, and not bring himself into difficulties by sparing a man who might make him repent of it when it would be too late.

Accordingly John was sent as a prisoner, out of Herod's suspicious temper, to Machaerus, the castle I already mentioned, and was put to death. Now the Jews thought that the destruction of his army was sent as a punishment upon Herod, and a mark of God's displeasure with him.

Appendix 2: The Fortress of Machaerus, from Chapter Six of Josephus' Jewish War, trans. Whiston

. . . for the nature of the place was very capable of affording the surest hopes of safety to those that possessed it, as well as delay and fear to those that should attack it; for what was walled in was itself a very rocky hill, elevated to a very great height; which circumstance alone made it very hard to be subdued. It was also so contrived by nature, that it could not be easily ascended; for it is, as it were, ditched about with such valleys on all sides, and to such a depth, that the eye cannot reach their bottoms, and such as are not easily to be passed over, and even such as it is impossible to fill up with earth. For that valley which cuts it on the west extends to threescore furlongs, and did not end till it came to the lake Asphaltites; on the same side it was also that Machaerus had the tallest top of its hill elevated above the rest. But then for the valleys that lay on the north and south sides, although they be not so large as that already described, yet it is in like manner an impracticable thing to think of getting over them; and for the valley that lies on the east side, its depth is found to be no less than a hundred cubits. It extends as far as a mountain that lies over against Machaerus, with which it is bounded.

Now when Alexander [Janneus], the king of the Jews, observed the nature of this place, he was the first who built a citadel here, which afterwards was demolished by Gabinius, when he made war against Aristobulus. But when Herod came to be king, he thought the place to be worthy of the utmost regard, and of being built upon in the firmest manner, and this especially because it lay so near to Arabia;

for it is seated in a convenient place on that account, and hath a prospect toward that country; he therefore surrounded a large space of ground with walls and towers, and built a city there, out of which city there was a way that led up to the very citadel itself on the top of the mountain; nay, more than this, he built a wall round that top of the hill, and erected towers at the corners, of a hundred and sixty cubits high; in the middle of which place he built a palace, after a magnificent manner, wherein were large and beautiful edifices.

Select Bibliography

Chancey, Mark A.: *Greco-Roman Culture and the Galilee of Jesus*, Cambridge, 2005

Evans, Craig A.: *Jesus and His World*, SPCK, 2012

Freyne, Seán: *Galilee from Alexander the Great to Hadrian*, T&T Clark, 1998

Grant, Robert M.: *A Historical Introduction to the New Testament*, Collins, 1963

Green, Joel B.: *The Gospel of Luke*, Eerdmans, 1997

Holum, Kenneth G. et al: *King Herod's Dream: Caesarea on the Sea*, Norton, 1987

James, M.R. (trans.): *The Apocryphal New Testament*, Oxford, 1953

Jones, A.H.M.: *The Herods of Judaea*, Oxford, 1938

Josephus: *Jewish Antiquities*, Wordsworth, 2006

Josephus: *The Jewish War*, Penguin, 1959

Lindars, Barnabas: *John*, JSOT, 1990

Marshall, Alfred (ed.): *The Interlinear Greek-English New Testament*, Samuel Bagster, 1959

Pfeiffer, Robert H: *History of New Testament Times*, Adam and Charles Black, 1949

Philo Judaeus (trans. Charles Yonge): *Works*, Bohn, 1854-5

Plutarch: *The Fall of the Roman Republic*, Penguin, 1972

Pummer, Reinhard: *The Samaritans: A Profile*, Eerdmans, 2016

Rieu, E.V. (trans.): *The Four Gospels*, Penguin, 1952

Ritmeyer, Leen and Kathleen: *Jerusalem in the Year 30 AD*, Carta, 2015

Roberts, Alexander and Donaldson, James (eds.): *The Anti-Nicene Fathers* Vol VIII, Eerdmans, 1951

Smallwood, E. Mary: *The Jews Under Roman Rule*, Brill, 2001

Suetonius: *The Twelve Caesars*, Penguin, 2003

Tacitus: *Annals*, Oxford, 2008

Webb, Simon: *What Do We Know About Pontius Pilate?* Langley Press, 2018

Wilde, Oscar: *The Plays of Oscar Wilde*, Wordsworth, 2002

Wilde, Oscar: *Salome*, John Lane, 1907

Wroe, Ann: *Pilate: The Biography of an Invented Man*, Jonathan Cape, 1999

Some Feature Films Mentioned in the Text (Director, Title, Date)

DeMille, Cecil B.: *The King of Kings*, 1927

Gibson, Mel: *The Passion of the Christ*, 1927

Jewison, Norman: *Jesus Christ Superstar*, 1973

Koster, Henry: *The Robe*, 1953

Pasolini, Pier Paulo: *The Gospel of Matthew*, 1964

Ray, Nicholas: *King of Kings*, 1961

Reynolds, Kevin: *Risen*, 2016

Welles, Orson: *Citizen Kane*, 1941

Wyler, William: *Ben-Hur*, 1959

For free downloads and more from the Langley Press,
please visit our website at

http://tinyurl.com/lpdirect